Through the Eye of a Needle

Through the Eye of a Needle

Carol Harper

Tate Publishing & *Enterprises*

TATE PUBLISHING
& *Enterprises*

Tate Publishing is committed to excellence in the publishing industry. Our staff of highly trained professionals, including editors, graphic designers, and marketing personnel, work together to produce the very finest books available. The company reflects the philosophy established by the founders, based on Psalms 68:11,

"THE LORD GAVE THE WORD AND GREAT WAS THE COMPANY OF THOSE WHO PUBLISHED IT."

If you would like further information, please contact us:
1.888.361.9473 | www.tatepublishing.com
TATE PUBLISHING & *Enterprises*, LLC | 127 E. Trade Center Terrace
Mustang, Oklahoma 73064 USA

Through the Eye of a Needle
Copyright © 2007 by Carol Harper. All rights reserved.

No part of this publication may be reproduced, stored in a retrieval system or transmitted in any way by any means, electronic, mechanical, photocopy, recording or otherwise without the prior permission of the author except as provided by USA copyright law.

Scripture quotations marked "KJV" are taken from the Holy Bible, King James Version, Cambridge, 1769. Used by permission. All rights reserved.

The opinions expressed by the author are not necessarily those of Tate Publishing, LLC.

This book is designed to provide accurate and authoritative information with regard to the subject matter covered. This information is given with the understanding that neither the author nor Tate Publishing, LLC is engaged in rendering legal, professional advice. Since the details of your situation are fact dependent, you should additionally seek the services of a competent professional.

Book design copyright © 2007 by Tate Publishing, LLC. All rights reserved.
Cover & Interior design by Chris Webb

Published in the United States of America

ISBN: 978-1-5988686-5-4

06.11.10

To my husband, David
Who took me by the hand and showed me
That life was meant to be lived in love and happiness.

To my daughter, Rachelle
Who taught me that life is precious,
Never to be taken advantage of.

To my son, Kevin
Who taught me that life can be tough,
But that the strength of spirit moves you forward.

To my father, Charles
Who taught me that love can be shown
Without a word having to be said.

To my mother, Thelma, God rest her soul,
Who showed me what pure fortitude can do.

To my grandmother, Doris
Who, for over forty years,
never ceased to pray for my salvation.

To my Savior, Jesus Christ, My Lord, and My God,
Who taught me everything I know,
And everything I ever knew.

Table of Contents

Prologue: The Story   9

Chapter 1: The Question: What Shall I Do?   13

Chapter 2: The Same Question: What Shall I Do?   21

Chapter 3: The Needle's Eye   31

Chapter 4: Common Grounds   49

Chapter 5: Unorthodox Christianity   89

Epilogue: The Journey   119

Prologue: The Story

For thirty years, I was an active member of the Church of Jesus Christ of Latter-day Saints (LDS, the Mormons), commercially known as a good, moral, family-based religion. One of the richest religions in the world with assets in the billions and billions, Mormonism's history, theology and doctrines are labyrinths of complexity. The LDS church is also authoritative and dominated by a priesthood hierarchy. If one is familiar with their TV commercials or the marketed pitches programmed into and rehearsed by young men with black name tags—it goes to reason that one should deeply investigate and dig deeper than Mormonism's shiny surface before proceeding to the waters of an LDS baptism.

Out of the frying pan and into the fire, I entered mainstream Christianity, full-throttle. I've separated my being born again and my experiences in Christianity as two totally different events because, ironically, I often find them in conflict with each other. Some churches were way too big, like the LDS church, the magnitude of belief systems and statements seemed just as complex as Mormonism's. Others were small and struggling just to get by, often closing down for lack of both congregational and monetary support, and just as in the LDS church, I found way too many politics, hypocrisy and rampant wrongful judgments being made. I walked out of many a sincere, passionately delivered sermon almost hoping someone would be watching and follow suit. No one ever did. Like a wandering Goldilocks, I wondered if I'd ever find a church that was "just right." Confused by the varying belief systems, segregation of the denominations, and cultures of Christianity—ironically feeling like Joseph Smith in his purported "First Vision" story—I had come to the brink of losing faith; not in the sheep, but in the shepherds and stewards who took it upon themselves to be in charge of Christ's flocks. It wasn't that they weren't getting fed (John 21: 15–17); it was *what* they were being fed that kept me at bay.

I have been asked several times what it was like to leave an organized religion such as Mormonism. It has certainly been an amazing journey that has been both spiritually and emotionally hard to convey. What many don't realize is the same harrowing experience of leaving the LDS church obliged me to examine the themes and variations of today's mainstream Christianity. So, for as many that have asked, my answer is beautifully illustrated in the nineteenth chapter of the Gospel of Matthew—a dialogue between Jesus Christ himself and a rich young man:

> And behold, one came and said unto him, Good master, what good thing shall I do, that I may have eternal life?

> And he said unto him, Why callest thou me good? There is none good but one, that is, God; but if thou wilt enter into life, keep the commandments.

> He saith unto him, Which?
> Jesus said, Thou shalt do no murder, Thou shalt not

commit adultery, Thou shalt not steal, Thou shalt not
bear false witness, Honour thy father and thy mother:
and, Thou shalt love they neighbour as thyself.

The young man saith unto him, All these things have I
kept from my youth up: what lack I yet?

Jesus said unto him, If thou wilt be perfect,
go and sell that thou hast, and give to the poor,
and thou shalt have treasure in heaven:
and come, follow me.

But when the young man heard that saying, he went
away sorrowful: for he had great possessions.
Then said Jesus unto his disciples, Verily I say unto you,
That a rich man shall hardly enter into the kingdom
of heaven.

And again, I say unto you, It is easier for a camel to go
through the eye of a needle, than for a rich man to enter
into the kingdom of God.

When his disciples heard it, they were exceedingly
amazed, saying, Who then can be saved?

But Jesus beheld them and said unto them,

With men this is impossible; but with God all things
are possible.

Then answered Peter and said unto him,
Behold, we have forsaken all, and followed thee;
what shall we have therefore?

And Jesus said unto them, Verily I say unto you,
That ye which have followed me, in the regeneration
when the Son of man shall sit in the throne of his glory,
ye also shall sit upon twelve thrones, judging the twelve
tribes of Israel.

And everyone that hath forsaken houses, or brethren,
or sisters, or father, or mother, or wife, or children, or
lands, for my name's sake, shall receive an hundredfold,
and shall inherit everlasting life.

But many that are first shall be last; and the last shall
be first.

Matthew 19: 16–28

ONE

THE QUESTION: WHAT SHALL I DO?

In the arid deserts of Judea, a wealthy young man approaches Jesus Christ with a question:

> Good master, what good thing shall I do, that I may have eternal life?

This young man may have acquired his riches by working hard and saving for many years. Or, perhaps it took a lot of strategic thinking to achieve his status; maybe he obtained a rich inheritance. It doesn't say *how* his riches were attained, but it does say he had "great possessions." Of course, what was "great" about what he possessed is not defined either, but we do know Jesus eventually makes His point to His disciples, so obviously this man is known to be well–off.

It is possible that this young man may have had his answer formulated even before asking his question of the "good master." Was he personally acquainted with the man he had the honor of approaching and addressing? Not only that, any number of indicators could have given away that a rich man was in the crowd—the clothes he wore, the way he carried himself, an entourage of friends and admirers. In fact, Jesus probably saw this man coming.

So the Master of the teaching moment responds:

> Why callest thou me good?
> There is none good but one, that is, God;
> but if thou wilt enter into life,
> keep the commandments.

Jesus essentially answers the question with a question: Why are you calling me good? How do you know I'm good? This rich man was one of hundreds, perhaps thousands who had heard of or knew something about Jesus, but in all actuality didn't know Him any better than the next guy. Certainly not like His own disciples knew Him. So how would he know to call Christ "good," much less "master"?

Jesus corrects him by focusing on God. God is good—on that you can rely, and proceeds to give him the answer: keep the commandments. To which the young man replies:

> He saith unto him, Which?

Good question! Which of *ten*, or which of the entire Judaic Law? In the interest of time, it appears that Jesus gives him a little review:

> Jesus said, Thou shalt do no murder, Thou shalt not commit adultery, Thou shalt not steal, Thou shalt not bear false witness, Honour thy father and thy mother: and, Thou shalt love thy neighbour as thyself.

Love. I find it interesting that in this brief Decalogue of "thou shalt nots . . ." Jesus slips in love—something "thou shalt *do*." Have you ever noticed that today, in the popularly recited, posted, and framed Exodus 20 Ten Commandments, the word "love" is often excluded? Yet love is certainly the running theme of Jesus' entire ministry: Love God, love your neighbor, even love your enemies.

What Do I Lack?

> The young man saith unto him, All these things have I kept from my youth up: what lack I yet?

If this young man were honest with himself and those within ear shot, he'd save some face and realize not only is no one perfect (save God), but no one—the entire Sanhedrin, the most Orthodox Jew, even Moses himself—had or ever could live the entire Judaic Law perfectly and completely. However, the person standing right in front of him, Jesus Christ, was the very fulfillment of this man's claim to fame.

Was this young man prideful or naïve enough to think he didn't lack anything else than what he already had, past or present? Did he honestly believe he had it all and was not only well-off, but also well versed in the laws, customs and beliefs of Judaism? That one could be so fortunate and blessed to believe this about one's self! Even if he had done his very best to keep his perfection and goodness up from his youth, deficient in seemingly nothing at all, the fact that he had to approach Jesus for validation shows he had a slight degree of arrogant immaturity. That, along with material goods that authenticated a life of success, would surely seem that the only thing he felt he lacked was the approval of the Rabbi, which he ambitiously sought that day.

> Then Jesus beholding him loved him . . . (Mark 10: 21)

Jesus, giving him the benefit of the doubt, loves him. This young man has definitely pleased Him—that there would be one so pure and untainted as to wonder what he lacked to attain eternal life. Jesus, with love and in a non-condescending manner, gives him the answer:

The Answer: What To Do

Matthew 19:21
Jesus said unto him, If thou wilt be perfect, go and sell that thou hast, and give to the poor, and thou shalt have treasure in heaven: and come, follow me.

Mark 10: 21
One thing thou lackest: go thy way, sell whatever thou hast, and give to the poor. and thou shalt have treasure in heaven: and come, take up thy cross and follow me.

Between these two gospel versions, we can get the entire idea of what Christ is saying: *Sell* what you have; *give* to the poor; you'll have treasure in heaven. Oh yeah, and come *follow* me.

But wait a minute. That doesn't sound like one thing, that sounds like three: Sell, give, and follow me. You mean to tell me have to sell all of my stuff? Give it to the poor? Leave everything and follow you? And whoa, wait a minute . . . what cross?

I can almost hear the wheels turning in his head, the jaw drop, the short circuit, fork-in-the-road sigh. None of the three things Jesus required of this young man called for recited scripture, a Talmud test, or an overview of Jewish Law and doctrine; nor was any sort of sacrifice, ritual or ceremonial tidbit essential to supporting his claim of progressive perfection from his youth until that very moment, even though it may have been what he was prepared with. He may have already had his response on the tip of his tongue, primed to respond to any answer but the one he heard: give up everything you have—even the very life as you know it—and follow me.

> But when the young man heard that saying,
> he went away sorrowful: for he had great possessions.

He just couldn't do it, and he *didn't* do it. For some reason, perhaps for more than one, this wealthy man refused to take that leap of faith to find out what could possibly be beyond the sacrifice of what he already possessed. He was unable to give up his riches and blessings, well-versed intellect, home, family and friends, life—to give it all away and follow the One who had promised him treasure in heaven. It would nearly cause one to speculate which of his greatest possessions took more precedence over the greater promise of eternal life.

The Eye of A Needle

> Then said Jesus unto his disciples, Verily I say unto you, That a rich man shall hardly enter into the kingdom of heaven.

> And again, I say unto you, It is easier for a camel to go

through the eye of a needle, than for a rich man to enter into the kingdom of God.

(A note in the Bible's NIV translation states: *The camel was the largest animal found in the Holy Land. The vivid contrast between the largest animal and the smallest opening represents what, humanly speaking, is impossible.*)

As proverbial as it most likely was in Jesus' time, it still evokes a visual that surpasses understanding: a camel, which often carried a traveler's entire load of necessities and possessions, livelihood and trade in caravans loaded with goods, spices, etc., going through the eye of a needle. Then again, large things passing through small openings aren't that impossible. No one says, upon seeing a pregnant woman, "How on earth are you going to get that baby out?" An octopus can fit through an opening as wide as their beak. How do they get those model ships into glass bottles? My cats can finagle themselves into crevices and spaces I never thought possible. From a single backpack, an entire parachute can open wide to bring a skydiver safely down.

In one simple statement, Jesus' camel-and-needle analogy revealed both the certainties and uncertainties of what is possible and impossible. A statement that caused his disciples to wonder: *who then can be saved?*

Indeed, who? This question the disciples tossed among themselves was perhaps the one that the young man *should* have asked of Jesus. But the event had happened, the story has been told. This rich young man—who had the privilege of standing in front of the Savior of the world for a brief moment in time, unwilling to shed his riches, his belongings, his very life as he knew it—went his way, sorrowfully rejecting the challenge.

Who then can be saved? Not that young man. Not that day. All the tangible treasures of his own little world kept him in a bubble, afraid to search for a greater treasure unseen. Even with the loving encouragement from the only One who could save him, he still could not find it in his heart to forsake the comforts of his possessions to follow Jesus through the needle's eye.

But what if he had?

TWO

THE SAME QUESTION: WHAT SHALL I DO?

Good master, what good thing shall I do, that I may have eternal life?

Though the source or acquisition of the young man's riches couldn't be determined in the story, mine could be easily delineated. The LDS church was my life—in fact, it was one of my greatest possessions. My family, the LDS communities I lived in, my friends, my testimony of the restored LDS Gospel—I was richly blessed with everything I could ever ask for. I had a great family and parents who loved me and supported my talents and endeavors at a very early age. All my needs were filled. I was well-off by so many standards.

If I could tell you what being raised in the LDS church was like in one sentence: It was a good thing. I was blessed and sealed in the LDS temple as an adopted infant to my parents. I went through Primary and was baptized at the age of eight. I was active in Mutual and Young Women's all throughout my teen years. I didn't smoke, I didn't drink, and I didn't swear—much. I dressed modestly. I read and studied the LDS scriptures diligently, attended and graduated from early-morning Seminary. There were pictures of temples and books by LDS authors, and LDS magazines such as *Church News, Ensign,* and *The New Era* everywhere in our home. My father served in quite a few priesthood capacities and was a wonderful example to me as a very good man. My mother was active in the Relief Society, and taught me how to cook, bake, sew, plant, raise and harvest a garden, can, dehydrate and freeze food, and a host of other homemaking skills. My parents even required me to take W. Cleon Skousen's National Center for Constitutional Studies course at an early age. My entire family was heavily involved and key players in the "Second Rescue" project of the Willie's Handcart Company. My brother served an honorable LDS mission in San Jose, California, and a couple of my nephews served missions in London and San Diego. I rarely missed a Stake or General Conference. I was definitely your average Molly Mormon—the LDS church was my world.

I attended Brigham Young University where I met a returned missionary and we married in the Salt Lake City temple nearly a year later. I was only nineteen years old. We lived in Provo, Utah, in the BYU family housing just off campus, and I worked just minutes away in Springville. A year later my son was born, and a year later, my daughter. My then husband eventually graduated with an MBA from BYU's Marriott School of Management.

With the majority of my callings being music related, I did pretty well as an LDS musician in Utah. I once arranged and directed the music, choir and children's choir for a BYU fireside where Gordon B. Hinckley was the keynote speaker before he was called as President/Prophet. I met Hinckley and his entourage in the green room before the performance. Jeffrey Holland, then the President of BYU, and his wife commented that it was the first time they knew of a children's choir performing at a BYU fireside. At the BYU Motion Picture Studios, I sat in on a couple mix-down/mastering sessions with Marie Osmond's husband on one of her Christmas specials. I met Kurt Bestor, co-composer of the music for Salt Lake City's 2002 Olympics, and sat in on a couple of his projects at Rosewood Studios in Orem, Utah. It was shortly after this that I began composing and arranging LDS music.

After my husband graduated with his MBA, our family moved out to California where I continued to do music for the LDS church. The callings I had were, again, music related except for once, when I served as a ward Relief Society secretary. I composed and submitted music for the *Ensign* Music Contests every year and was a four-time winner. I even had the privilege of hearing one of my songs performed in Temple Square in Salt Lake City. At a reception afterward in the Joseph Smith Memorial Building, I met LDS Music Chairman Michael Moody, and well-known LDS composer Janice Kapp Perry. I wrote a Christmas cantata and an Easter cantata—both of which were performed at the Oakland Temple—and had begun writing an oratorio entitled *Israel!* The ward choir I directed was Paul Anka's backup choir for his finale piece during one of his performances at the Mountain Winery in Saratoga. I composed, arranged and played for many LDS events: baptisms, wedding receptions, Relief Society functions and ward and stake conferences. I composed and arranged music for most any LDS function.

I went to the Oakland temple as often as I could, paid my tithing, followed the Word of Wisdom (Mormon health code), and observed the Sabbath Day. I attended Relief Society homemaking meetings. I faithfully fulfilled all callings the Bishopric had assigned me. I had the missionaries over for dinner once a month, and even played a part in the baptisms of a few converts. We had Visiting Teachers and Home Teachers over most every month, and I myself was a Visiting Teacher. Our family frequently held Family Home Evenings. I loved every single ward I was in. By the book, I was as active as anyone could be in the LDS church. I never had to ask the question, "What shall I do to gain eternal life?" I already knew the answer—*I was living it!* I had been raised in it; I was doing it, had it handed to me, laid out for me from the very day I was sealed to my parents as a baby. Every detail of my life was planned, organized, influenced and often accomplished by the LDS church. This was my bubble, my life as I knew it. I trod the road of eternal progression as laid out for me "from my youth up." I could therefore, in good conscience, ask the question:

What Do I Lack?

> The young man saith unto him, All these things have I
> kept from my youth up: what lack I yet?

If I were honest with myself, and everyone at the time, I may have attempted to save face, realizing that no one—the LDS Prophet and General Authorities, the most Orthodox Mormon, even Joseph Smith or Brigham Young themselves—could live every detail of the Mormon religion perfectly. But it didn't really matter, anyway. Mormonism's systemized repentance process always seemed to have me back on the road to "eternal progression" in no time.

So what did I lack? By many standards, it would appear that I lacked nothing at all. In all reality, why would I ever think of ever asking such a question? I didn't and didn't have to. Did I honestly believe that I had it all, and was not only well-off, but also well-versed in the laws, customs and beliefs of Mormonism?

One day this was all laid out in front of me when I discovered that the shiny, squeaky clean life I was so busy living and loving—the road of eternal progression that I had been so diligently treading—paled greatly in comparison to the intriguing challenge Jesus Christ offered. None of the three things Jesus required of me called for recited scripture from the LDS Quad, a test on Mormon theology and doctrine, or the recitative of the 13 Articles of Faith. Nor were any of the ceremonial rituals I had performed countless times in the LDS temples essential to supporting my claim of progressive perfection from my youth until that very moment, even though I was fully prepared with all of it. I already had my responses. My testimony had always been on the tip of my tongue, primed from my youth to respond to any answer but the one I wanted to hear: sell everything you have.

It was if Christ were standing in front of me with the choice: Follow me? Or follow Mormonism?

It all happened one day in early March, 1996. My then husband had come home from work, slowly walking up to front porch, his face white as a sheet and a demeanor so grave that I asked, "Oh my gosh, who died?" He proceeded to beckon me into the bedroom, closed the door, then broke down and said, "I can't be a Mormon anymore." And I sat stunned as he related the events of his day.

He had been sitting at his desk at work during lunch and had typed the word "Mormon" in the Internet search engine. Back then the Internet was nothing like it is today, but still, a myriad of sites came up, with one in particular catching his eye. He hesitantly clicked on it, and contained in the site were stories of those who had left the LDS church. One link led to another, and he sat there in shock as he painfully read through each site he happened upon.

By the time he was done, he knew he was out of Mormonism. His boss was understanding and allowed him to take the rest of the day off. He tried maintaining his composure until he was out of the office building, then he got into his car and broke down into sobs during the commute home. By the time he walked up to the house that afternoon, he looked like the living dead. His life in Mormonism—life as he knew it—was what had died that day.

Numbed by his story, I sat on the bed, not believing what I was hearing. He continued to cry, saying, "You can divorce me, you can leave me, move out. I don't want you to . . . I'm not telling you what you should do . . . I don't know what to do . . ." His broken voice trailed off into more sobs.

I sat and listened to him try to explain through mumbles and sobs. I was still numb and speechless—nothing prepares you for these types of bombshell moments, and I didn't know how to react. I eventually gathered enough of my thoughts together to ask him what it is he read. He immediately said no, that he didn't want to share specifics—as if, along with the associated pain and suffering, he wanted to protect me from what he had just been through. Fair enough.

That night I had a very hard time sleeping. I stared at the ceiling in the dark, trying to sort through the events of the day. I was not happy in this marriage, so among the dizzying options swirling around in my head I thought that now could be my chance. I would be justified in divorcing him and the church would be behind me in granting me a temple divorce. *This may be an inadvertent answer to prayer*, I thought.

However, that line of thinking didn't resolve one serious persistent thought that had equal mind share as I stared at the ceiling above me: *What did he read?* I faded off to a restless sleep with that question echoing in my mind.

The next day I scurried the kids off to school. Before he left for work, I came out and announced that I wanted to know what he read. He was still very reluctant and still very shaken from the day previous, but I told him that if he made a decision for himself that affected our lives like this, I had a right to know. He finally said that if I really wanted to know, he would print out some of what he read and bring it home from work that evening. I agreed.

After he left, I sat down in front of my computer and piano keyboard. I had been arranging and composing music for the ward Easter program, so I brought up the manuscript in my notation program and sat for a good ten minutes just staring at the blank staff template. I put my head down on the desk and kept asking myself, "What do I do?" over and over. I thought of my two kids, my friends, my family and I was scared about the future. But what I was more scared about was that I never thought about *me*. What do I think? What do I believe? What is it I fear?

I raised my head. *Wait a minute*, I thought. *I have a testimony of this church! I know this church is the only true one. I will write that testimony of mine, and it will be better than anything he read yesterday. And everything will be okay—I can continue composing music for the church, the kids will come home from school, I'll make dinner and our lives will be back to normal.*

I brought up the word processing program and started writing the testimony forged throughout my life since childhood: *I know this church is true, I know that Joseph Smith was a prophet of God, I know that . . .* I stopped and looked at what I had typed, and deleted it. That sounded like every testimony ever given! No, if I would change his mind and would be competing with anti-Mormon material, I need to be more convincing than the average testimony. I would write the best testimony ever and give it to him when he got home, in exchange for his reading material.

I started again. Deleted it. Started again. Deleted it. I couldn't believe that I couldn't even write my own testimony—one I had given countless times in fast and testimony meetings, at firesides, at the end of sacrament meeting talks. What was *wrong* with me? I searched my mind and heart for every reason why I couldn't at least write *something*. As the day wore on, I wondered if I knew anything at all about the church I professed to "know" was true. I felt bad, second-guessing my own testimony, which I had always felt was strong, even powerfully revealed through music I wrote for the church. But now I felt so much pressure, knowing that testimony was soon to be under the gun. I prayed that, though I couldn't write it, that I would be able to eloquently deliver that testimony when the time came.

So the computer screen sat blank all day, and before I knew it, he was home with a stack of papers more than an inch thick. He asked, "Are you sure?" I told him I just wanted to read it straight through with no interruptions or side comments. He obliged, and I commenced reading.

I scoffed through the first few pages, as they rang with the familiar "anti-Mormon" ravings I had heard about through the years, and I hastily shed each page. But as I continued to read, it began to feel as if my brain was being peeled apart like an onion, layer by layer, for as I scrutinized the subject matter before me, the pages began to fall slower, my derision turned to silence and my fears came to the forefront of my mind. I could feel the blood from my face drain to my stomach.

After reading the last page, I put the entire stack down, more stunned than I was the day previous. I looked up and whispered, "What are we going to do?" He just said, "I don't know . . . I don't know." And we wept, as we knew our lives would never be the same.

The Answer: What To Do

Matthew 19:21
Jesus said unto him, If thou wilt be perfect, go and sell that thou hast, and give to the poor, and thou shalt have treasure in heaven: and come, follow me.

Mark 10: 21
One thing thou lackest: go thy way, sell whatever thou hast, and give to the poor, and thou shalt have treasure in heaven: and come, take up thy cross and follow me.

Not many who believe that they truly have it all take the time to stop and consider what it is they spiritually lack. But for one important day of my entire life, I did take the time to stop and consider. After a long, painful, agonizing investigation of the origins, history, and yes, the very tainted, weak foundations that so deeply scratched the surface of Mormonism's polished exterior—a religion that I held most dear and had consumed my entire life up until those moments of truth—I found myself at the same fork in the road the rich young man chose to walk away from. Do I go the seemingly "safe" route? Or do I step out into the great unknown? The answer that was right in front of me—Jesus Christ—would prove to be the very fulfillment of a life slowly dying in front of my very eyes, awaiting rebirth. I just didn't know it yet.

> But when the young man heard that saying,
> he went away sorrowful: for he had great possessions.

Like this young man, I too, became sorrowful. Not just because the value of what I considered my greatest possession—Mormonism—had seriously declined, but also because I knew I had to forsake life as I knew it to take my first steps of faith in a desperate pursuit of truth. Yes, it would hurt. In fact, it would prove excruciatingly painful. It felt impossible, and sometimes I wanted to go back rather than endure it. But once I had started, I knew I could never go back, no more than a baby could be stuffed back into the womb that bore it. The water had broken, and after thirty years of labor, the time had come—

I was being born again through the eye of the needle.

> Except a man be born again
> he cannot see the kingdom of God . . .
> John 3:3

THREE

THE NEEDLE'S EYE

Jesus said unto him,
If thou wilt be perfect, go and sell that thou hast . . .

Challenge #1: Go and Sell What You Have
The Garage Sale

It would be very difficult for someone to just up and decide to sell all of his possessions. Was this really what Jesus asked of this young man? He told him "sell that thou hast." That would be . . . well, everything! This action alone would be a tough thing to do.

You don't have to be economically rich to have great possessions, for *"where your treasure is, there will your heart be also,"* (Matthew 6:21). To have been richly blessed in other areas than monetary can suffice for many. By pecuniary standards, I've never been rich by any stretch of the imagination, but as illustrated in the previous chapter, my life had been richly blessed by means of religious comforts. The LDS Church provided everything for me: a life, positions and callings, a worldwide family, a belief and support system, even welfare nets should I have ever needed to draw upon them. I have never known poverty, but I definitely knew what it was like to be "poor in spirit." Quite frankly, I don't know which is worse, but I can tell you this: both plead for a great amount of compassion and love.

Speaking of riches, in proceeding through the needle's eye, one of the not-so-big hurts was the realization of the thousands of dollars of tithing donated to the church via ten percent of one's annual income. Figuring that I should just cut my losses, I had never insisted on an itemization of where my tithing dollars went. I had always trusted the LDS Church to dole the money out judiciously via various channels through which they corporately invested. Even if I had demanded one, I sincerely doubt they could have followed my donations, dollar for dollar, and provided an accurate accounting of where my money actually went. Having a colossal entity such as The Corporation of the Church of Jesus Christ of Latter-Day Saints assume the responsibility of deciding where billions of tithing dollars go provides a convenience in allowing the general LDS membership shed responsibility and separate themselves from having to deal with or engage directly with "the poor."

Have you ever had a massive garage sale, and in the process of gathering everything, come to realize just how much stuff had been accumulated and saved over the years? My new husband, David, and I decided to have a garage sale one summer, and realized we had a massive clean up job in front of us. The first thing we did was take a survey of what we had, and just couldn't believe the amount of stuff! We went through cupboards, drawers, closets, the entire house and garage—finding and gathering up all sorts of things. Things, things, things! Things I didn't even know we had. Things I couldn't believe I had purchased, things I thought were lost, but I'd end up finding that we had two or three of the *same item*! Things I had bought and didn't even want or need in the first place. Things I wanted to keep, but just didn't work anymore or needed repair. Things that I'd look at, scratch my head and ask, "What *is* this?"

We had a clearinghouse of large proportions, selling as much as we could in a garage sale, and taking a good percentage of the remainder of things to the local charity store. The rest took four dump runs, and even after all was said and done; I'm sure we could have done another survey and found a lot more.

I'll never forget the feeling of finally being able to walk through the garage without tripping, how it felt to be able to actually find something in a cupboard or closet. There's nothing like cleaning house and simplifying life—sweeping away the cobwebs and dust, realizing one can do most definitely do without so much stuff! Once my house was clean, I found I had a desire to keep it that way—not fill it up again with junk I didn't need. The whole experience also helped me think about future acquisitions a little more carefully.

Literal dust and cobwebs are not that different from the figurative ones. Not too much can fit through a needle's eye, so one must do a survey as to what must go and what can stay. As I surveyed the numerous elements of religious beliefs I'd clung to for so many years in both Mormonism *and* Christianity, I realized I could do without a lot of the "things" that had weighed me down. Things, things, things! Things I didn't even know I believed. Things I had bought into, that I didn't believe in the first place. Things I wanted to keep, but didn't work for me anymore, or just needed repair. Things that I'd look at, scratch my head and ask, "What *is* this?"

FOR SALE: *One religion. Everything must go—belief system, scriptures, icons, idols, statues, jewelry, temples, rituals, catch phrases, repetitious chants and mantras, recited prayers, clothes, etc. Delivery negotiable. Mind, heart and soul not included.*

So I had a *spiritual* garage sale; the rest went into many a virtual "dump run." My spiritual house was finally clean, but I wasn't about to fill it up again with junk that I didn't need. Most of all, the whole experience helped me think about future spiritual acquisitions a little more carefully.

Challenge #2: Giving to the Poor
Do It *Myself*

Back to the tithing dilemma—in hindsight, had I thought my "riches" through and taken inventory and responsibility of them *myself*—I would have taken that ten percent tithe out *myself* and placed it in an interest-accruing savings account *myself*. At the end of the month, or in December, when the LDS tithing settlement usually occurred, I would take out the money *myself*, go on the streets and give, give, give. I'd donate to homeless shelters *myself*. I'd donate to the charity or church of my choice *myself*; bring the cash or check down *myself*. I'd buy food and assemble food boxes to give out *myself*. I would have the money to give, when asked by someone who was down and out *myself*. Instead of being a missionary going door-to-door hoping to convert someone to a religion, I'd go door to door with the purpose of finding out what people *really* need—a meal, a prayer, someone to talk to, some companionship or maybe just someone who'll be there to listen.

I'd buy or donate clean coats and warm clothing, and give them out on the street corners *myself*. Pay for a shopping cart filled with groceries for a hungry family *myself*. Good stuff, too—not cheap canned yams, lima beans, or expired mac and cheese! I'd give of my time and talents to write resumes and fill out job applications for homeless job seekers, or babysit for homeless mothers while they job search, or talk to abused women. I'd read a book to the bedridden, sit and have coffee with a co-worker who's having a bad day. And I'd do this all *myself*. *Directly*. Eye to eye contact. Smiles and hugs are free! The Good Samaritan being not just a good story, but the rule.

Can you imagine how the world would be changed if not just I, but everyone did that?

Now, could you imagine what would happen if the LDS Church sold everything—all of its assets, its astounding wealth in the billions upon billions—and did the same? Sell everything: their properties—yes, even the ones that the beautiful ornate temples sit on, take all of the tithed money they've ever received, including all interest accrued; maybe even build houses for the poor right where those gold-trimmed temples once sat. How much does it cost for one temple to be built? Why not use that money and give it to the poor instead? Perhaps the Mormon church could even open their ward buildings for a soup line or shelter, open storehouses to *everyone*. Just take all the billions and give it all away, like Scrooge on Christmas Day. *All* of it! Every month, every week, every day! No more funneling through those previously decided upon corporate charities, tossing out bones to the media as they shake hands with each other for the PR value. Just roll up their sleeves, get on the streets and start giving it all away!

Was Jesus actually saying that the money the rich man got from the proceeds of his "everything-must-go" estate sale goes to the poor? Yes, that's *exactly* what Jesus was saying. Giving to the poor was the very action He wanted the rich man to *directly feel* the benefits of—that *change-the-world* type of action. The power of loving compassion is an incredible thing, and He wanted him to feel that power directly. Eye to eye contact. What better way to experience the kingdom of heaven right here, right now? What action would be better to communicate the importance of one's worth? And if that rich young man sold all he had, wouldn't he then have been considered among the poor? Maybe, maybe not. Maybe that was the point; maybe it was the very thing he needed to feel in order to truly understand what it meant to be rich by heaven's standards, not earth's—that "one thing" he lacked:

. . . . and thou shalt have treasure in heaven . . .

Heaven. An after-life dimension that for many would be treasure enough in which to forever dwell. Jesus states plainly that this is promised, not imagined: thou shalt *have*. All actions of love would trigger and push towards that needle's eye: Go. Sell. Give.

. . . and come, follow me.

Challenge #3: Come, Follow Me
Leaving Religion Behind

I could understand the rich young man's dilemma, and cannot blame him for walking away in sorrow. This is a tough one. To forsake all elements of a former life for a new one that requires a complete leap of faith into unfamiliar territory seems like a rare, impossible challenge.

It certainly was for me. But rather than walk away from Jesus, I took the risk and forsook my old life in Mormonism, trusting in that promised treasure. And I understood what Christ meant when He said, "take up the cross." It is a lonely state of affairs when the people with whom you once associated and endeared reject you, mock you, gossip about you and call you an "apostate." In fact, it's a heavy cross to bear when you are misunderstood and ridiculed for forsaking the only life you ever knew just for the sake of searching for the truth.

Leaving a religion for doctrinal or theological reasons is an ominous challenge. In fact, it is very rare. Besides the obvious "how" and "why" questions that often hung in the air, I immediately had to endure an agonizing deprogramming process from LDS scripture, culture and protocol. It took everything in me to shed the elements of my ingrained culture and beliefs to actually think with my *own* brain, act with my *own* heart, see things with my *own* eyes, hear with new ears—a very painful process for one who had devoutly believed and even testified of those Mormon beliefs through her very gift of music.

There are two movies that help describe what my experience was like. *The Truman Show* is a good depiction of how the realization of a superficial life lived in supposed harmless deceit catches up with everyone in the end. It isn't love when one knowingly induces and convinces the unsuspecting and naïve to live or participate in a lie, no matter how well one is provided for. Let it suffice to say that the truth about Mormonism was revealed to me over the passage of time. However, the freedom that comes with knowing that truth didn't make it any easier to cope in a world I did not understand. Like Neo in the movie, *The Matrix*, as reality and truth ripped their way through a pseudo-life, there were countless times when I cried out, longing for the warm, familiar womb of Mormonism. The emotional pain was so great that I was seriously tempted with every call or visit from an LDS family member or friend, urging me to reconsider and come back. My social life literally fell apart.

The mental pain was anguish as I put thousands of pieces of a complex puzzle together, weeping as the true picture of Mormonism unfolded. Yet there was nothing and no one to whom I could cling to once those realizations set in. Physically, I endured exhausting periods of sobbing, throbbing headaches, occasional vomiting and disorientation as I watched my world and life dissolve around me. Sometimes all I could do was sit and cry through unexpected bouts that happened throughout an intense deprogramming process. But there was no going back. How could I, knowing now what I knew? Even if I had surrendered to an "ignorance is bliss" temptation—what I don't know about Mormonism couldn't hurt me—just how long could I have survived by maintaining a façade?

No, I would rather have known the truth and endured the excruciating pains associated with knowing it, than ever be content in living and continuing a lie.

> You shall know the truth, and the truth shall make you free.
> John 8:32

Shedding the guilt and fears that held me captive for so long took an amazing amount of courage. Taking off my temple garments and throwing them away was easier said than done when fears of lightening strikes or the possibility of something bad happening to me gripped my mind. It took me a while to deprogram and differentiate between Book of Mormon and actual Bible scripture; between Mormonism's fantasy and life's reality. I hadn't considered or even comprehended that miracles happen and prayers are answered to those outside the LDS church—miracles and prayers that Mormons often claim as proof that theirs is the only true church. Or even something as silly as considering that millions of people drink coffee every morning, have a glass of wine with dinner and don't wear "funny underwear," and *they're still alive!* Instead of others on the outside curiously looking in, I had been on the inside of the Mormon biosphere and was now stepping out. I discovered that there was a whole world going on outside the LDS bubble!

Akin to learning to walk for the first time, I had come to rely on the "belief legs" that had held me up for so long that my "faith legs" were extremely weak. Like a toddler in a big world of countless possibilities, it was God who would have to take me by the hand and teach me how to walk, sometimes carrying me in His arms for some pretty long stretches. There were even times when I refused to take His hand, thinking I could do all myself, angry, believing that God had abandoned me. I had even resigned myself to living this life all alone, before even learning how to walk in it. It took a few good hard falls for me to finally reach up and remember: "This time, *don't let go.*"

Perhaps sheer curiosity led me to realize the truth about a lot of things in my life, not just the spiritual aspects, for I eventually recognized that many decisions I had made in the past led me up to these moments of truth during my exit from Mormonism. The pattern wasn't always clear, but if I laid out a timeline of my former life, the events themselves would be undeniable, for I recognized little windows of truth revealed to me along the way. Problem was, I: 1) was unaware or oblivious to those revelations, 2) couldn't comprehend them at the time they happened, or 3) was so institutionalized that I had closed those windows, refusing to ever deal with them. In fact, I never had to deal with anything controversial or contrary to my belief system. The LDS church seemed to have the answers for everything. So why ever question it?

After leaving, I had absolutely nothing and no one, so I had to find the answers myself. It was like crawling through a desert, unsure if what I saw or experienced were mirages or the real thing. I only knew that I had to set my shaky feet upon the dusty path to find out. It was scary, but necessary. The pain I endured had embittered me to an agnostic or almost atheistic state. I hadn't thrown the baby out with the bathwater, but I came incredibly close. As I sat right in the middle of the ashes of a former life, my aching soul cried out, *Okay, if there is a God out there somewhere who even cares about me, then why would such a God cause this to happen to me?* I yearned for some comfort and peace from my anguish, mourning the loss of my Mormon friends and family who had abandoned and rejected me, who told me that I was going through hell because, "That's what you get when you leave the only true church on the face of the earth." I was truly alone, and at the same time I had a hole in my heart and soul that was greatly longing to be filled. So since I had just experienced the precious catalyst of freewill, I took advantage of that freedom and began to study the religions of the world.

At the time of my search the Internet was nothing like it is now, so I spent a lot of time checking out books from the Religion section of the local library. I started with Zen Buddhism and went through the entire gamut of world religions: Hinduism, Islam, Taoism—I studied whatever "-ism" was available to me in that library. I read holy books such as the Qur'an, the Bhagavada Gita, the Talmud, Veda, The Analects; I even researched Greek philosophy, Wicca and New Age ideologies. A friend of mine let me borrow a copy of her Urantia Book; another friend had me reading books about some lady who had life after death experiences. I skimmed through books on various cults and the occult, including Satanism. I explored my own Native American roots, hoping to find some sort of spiritual connection there. I studied the influential roles religion had played throughout world history. The librarian would smile every time I approached the counter to check out a stack of books and say, "Ah, yes—it's the religion lady!"

It was wonderful! I approached each book and subject with an intense eagerness. I was free! After all, I had nothing to lose. Trying to be objective in a search of subjective material was irrelevant.

No one was around to try to convince me of this way or that. The religious world was my oyster.

It was my eventual studies in Judaism that peaked my curiosity about the Messianic prophecies. Knowing already that Jews believe the Messiah is yet come, I also knew that Christians believe that the Messiah had not only already come, but would someday return. So the next logical step, at least to me at the time, seemed to be the study of Christianity. I had believed before that Mormonism was just another denomination as Christianity. Of course, I was quite mistaken, for if that were true, the transition from Mormonism to any denomination of mainstream Christianity wouldn't have been so horrendous. But I had come to find that there were stark contrasts between Joseph Smith's Jesus Christ, and the Jesus Christ as presented in the Gospels, so I had to undergo yet another deprogramming process to correct the confusion that seemed to continually plague my naiveté. Back to the library I went.

Born Again

I am the way, the truth, and the life . . .
John 14:6

I had already been quite skeptical about the Bible in general, and approached my studies of the Gospels in much the same way. I don't know, perhaps God had opened my mind a little *too* much, but I was very scrutinizing of the Bible. I even sparred with a few pastors. At the conclusion of one of these religious wrestles, one pastor in particular said to me, "The truth has set you free from the counterfeit scriptures, mythology and folklore of Mormonism, so it is only natural for you to apply the same kinds of tests to the

Bible. Theologically speaking, you are the kind of person I fear the most." Of course, his fear was unnecessary. But still, I felt then as I do now that *everyone* should be cautious and discerning about what they put their belief and trust in, especially anything deemed as scripture, no matter what the holy book.

It wasn't an alter call, a series of missionary lessons, a poignant TV commercial or film clip about families being forever, or "Another Testament of Jesus Christ," a lifestyle change, or a book or pamphlet. It wasn't a church I visited, nor any event or activity that was put on by any particular church or organization. It wasn't any one thing that someone said or did, trying to convince me that a witness of the truth was indicated by goose bumps, chills up the spine, "swelling motions" or a "burning in the bosom." It wasn't someone's testimony or vision that their "church was true." By this time I had learned how to guard my faith carefully, and I knew better than to rely on the playing on human emotion or dramatic presentations to dictate where my spiritual loyalties should lie.

No, I was alone when I came out the other side of the needle—when I was born again.

I was laying on my bed, dressed in a pair of sweats and a robe, reading a story in the ninth chapter of the Gospel of John about a man blind from birth who Jesus heals. By the time the story ended, I was weeping. All of my religious studies seemed to lead up to that very moment and culminate into an ultimate question that burned inside of me: *Who is God?* I knew who all these different religions *claimed* was God or gods: Allah, Buddha, Krishna, Yahweh, the Great Spirit. I knew all about the LDS doctrine concerning the Mormon God, or gods, more like. But now I found myself reading about a man who, almost two thousand years ago, claimed deity—a gutsy move amidst a generation of unbelievers. Ironically, a generation of which I, too, had found myself included.

I decided to get on my knees at the foot of my bed, and petition

God, and the first words out of my mouth were: "Who *are* You? Please be straight with me. If You really exist, it's only fair that You be the one to show me and no one else. I cannot see the path ahead of me, so heal me of my own blindness, just as you did for this man who was born blind. If You did it *then*, and You claimed to be God *then*, You can do it *now*. If You came down as God in the flesh, and healed this man—if there is any truth to this story, then You'll do it for me, and You'll do it right here, right now!"

What happened next was incredible. My ears rang, my eyes began to slowly tear up and I couldn't breathe. At first, I thought it was just another bout of sobs coming on, but then my surroundings had disappeared and my entire life flashed before my eyes. Everything that was stored in my brain's memory banks had scrolled back within nanoseconds—from that very moment back to my earliest childhood memories. The flashbacks happened so fast and intensely that I felt disoriented, as if some sort of virtual time machine had whisked me away on a thirty-year whirlwind tour of my life. I became a third-person observer of the recollections of people, places and events that had happened, along with all the pain, suffering, joys, successes, fears, and my choices bad and good. Many regrets surfaced as my brain raced through the memories—regrets that wounded me like a slug in the stomach or a slap in the face. I thought to myself, *This is it. This is what it's like to die. Maybe I am dying* . . . Then everything came to an abrupt stop as I felt these words pierce my soul: *Remember what you've learned.*

I drew a deep breath, as if I had been held underwater the entire time and then released. The droning ring in my ears had stopped, and I wiped my blurry, tear-filled eyes. Time stood still, and for the very first time, *I could see*. I cannot explain *how*, but I can explain *why* . . .

Purpose. I could see the *purpose* of my past and present pain and suffering. I could see the purpose of my thirty year blindness. And after living in a world of black and white, I could now see in color. I had not only been born again, but I had received the answer to my initial petition: *I now knew exactly who God was.*

I was on the other side of the needle. The most precious gifts that God gave me that day were not just the healing gift of sight as I had asked for, nor even the revelation of who He truly was in the person of Jesus Christ, but the purpose of *time. My* time. And now, an infinite God in control of *all* time, who had experienced a finite existence like mine, would be at the helm of my new and everlasting life.

The Journey Continues

After being born again, I was basically an infant as I explored the realm of mainstream Christianity. Visiting different Christian churches and denominations for the first time was quite an experience. As I initially "shopped" for a church, I felt carried away in the streams of varying cultures, lost in a sea of perhaps too many choices: Methodist, Presbyterian, Catholic, Lutheran, Non-denominational, Assemblies of God, Christian Science, Seventh-day Adventist, Baptist; even sub-denominations that included Freewill Baptist, Southern Baptist, Missouri Synod Lutheran, Evangelical Free, and the list goes on.

Ironically, Mormonism turned out to be just one of many of the faceless religions lost in the crowd. But for myself, I wasn't necessarily looking for a church that was "true." Rather, I was looking for love and acceptance by a community of people. What I needed the most was a new family who would unconditionally love and accept me, for the one that I had just exited from had woefully rejected me.

I eventually found a pretty good church not but a few miles

from home. Before I knew it, I found myself signing up for Bible studies, women's activities, attending retreats and conferences, dedicating my time and talents to the worship team and children's choirs. I began to compose again, and even recorded a CD. I toured and spoke at various churches and conferences, was interviewed on Christian radio about my exit from Mormonism, and was a guest speaker and singer at a convention along with renowned author and speaker, Josh McDowell.

During that time, it really didn't occur to me that, both culturally and socially, not too much had changed. My new church had great children's and youth programs; the congregation welcomed me with open arms. Perhaps the most refreshing change was that, instead of the slow, yawn-invoking LDS hymns with words altered to fit Mormon doctrine accompanied by a half-asleep organist and chorister—the worship music at many Christian churches was fun, lively and truly inspirational. As a musician, this was of great significance to me. Other than that, I leapt from Mormonism into mainstream Christianity without a hitch—or at least, at the time, any obvious ones. But it seemed that I had traded one religion for another.

For all the LDS church's "Families are Forever" propaganda, or Dr. Dobson's *Focus on the Family* series, I dove headfirst into my new life in mainstream Christianity without ever coming to grips with the many issues in my past and present personal life. Almost paralleling with my new Christian life were residual effects of a thirteen-year marriage plagued by domestic violence and abuse, awaiting resolution. Keeping up the façade of a perfect family over the years had weighed me down. Also diagnosed with both depression and Chronic Fatigue Syndrome, I struggled greatly in raising my children. Just getting out of bed in the morning was an insurmountable task. I also had Carpal Tunnel Syndrome to the point that I couldn't even hold an eating utensil. As a classical pianist, this was a crippling sentence. The condescension through the years perpetrated by my then husband, along with two suicide attempts, spurred me on to another fork in the road: *If I don't do something about this soon, I will die.*

So I made some significant decisions about my life, one of which included putting a divorce in motion. As a result, a new beginning in a life of love and happiness emerged. Initiating a metamorphosis from a depressed mess who could barely look at herself in the mirror, to a beautiful, bubbly person who found her smile and laughter again, I was able to miraculously acquire the energy to pop out of bed, ready and thankful for each new day. No more living a lie, no more debilitating illnesses, no more depression.

Jesus promised: *"Ask and ye shall receive; seek and ye shall find, knock and shall be opened unto you," (Matthew 7:7).* As usual, God had impeccable timing: along the way I met my soul mate and wonderful husband, David. When we moved away from the busyness of city life to the quiet retreat of our mountain home, I continued my spiritual journey, seeking a community of love and acceptance, never tiring of God's wisdom and teachings expounded by His Son, Jesus Christ in the Gospels.

There were, and still may be, some differences to work out with both my LDS and Christian family and friends—or at least those whom I thought were. As I've mentioned before, the common reaction by the general LDS membership to my departure from Mormonism was flat out rejection. Some did attempt to win me back; others judged me as the worst kind of apostate, since I had turned my back on the temple covenants. Stories made their way through the LDS gossip circuits. Some claim I left because I didn't want to wear the garments, or that there was some sin that caused me to be unable to live the commandments and teachings of the LDS church, that my testimony was weak and couldn't stand up when tested, that I had turned anti-Mormon, or "if you aren't a Mormon now, you never were." One ward member even told me, "I heard it was because you wanted to drink coffee." I surely must have been viewed as a lost soul, especially considering there were many who knew how active I was in the LDS church. Gossip has always been a cancer of truth.

It wasn't much better when I left my Christian church. I found it incredible that so many felt the need to pin some sort of scarlet letter on me in order to validate, or justify, their rejection of me. The thing is: I could *totally* understand why they'd do that—I had already been through it all before. I had to remember that people are judgmental because they themselves are weak and fearful; *". . . he that is without sin among you, let him cast a stone at her," John 8:7*. Besides, I figured that Christ himself was judged much more harshly by His very own people than I ever was or would be, so somehow I was able to take comfort in the fact that He knew and understood what I was going through, so I bore the persecution as best I could.

Hopefully, in time, everyone will understand the better offer I had to take. It wasn't easy to give up a religion like Mormonism, nor was it painless to realize that mainstream Christianity had a history of turning upon itself. Following Jesus and Jesus alone is a lonely path to trod—it is not that broad and wide path that so many knowingly or unknowingly go down. It's a very straight and narrow one that very few find. But I believe there is a reason and purpose for everything, and if we are all open and ready, the time will come where there will be no more division and exclusion, but a wonderful journey of love trod together on common grounds.

So let's do it!

> And everyone that hath forsaken houses, or brethren, or sisters, or father, or mother, or wife, or children, or lands, for my name's sake, shall receive an hundredfold, and shall inherit everlasting life.

FOUR

Common Grounds

> With men this is impossible; but with
> God all things are possible.

Not many Christians understand Mormonism, nor why their friends or family end up joining the LDS church. By the same token, many Mormons have a similar curiosity as to why anyone would ever even want to leave. So after my journey through the needle's eye, I found myself in a unique position as I was asked numerous times to "help" bring friends or family members out of Mormonism's biosphere, like I myself had done. But then the dilemma became, "Bring them out—and into what? Mainstream Christianity?"

I've often thought of how I could delicately approach Mormons who were questioning their faith, keeping in mind that my family was, and still is active Mormon, or potential converts who had questions about the LDS church that their missionaries could not answer, and not come off insensitive, angry, rebellious or "anti-Mormon." It was a delicate fence walk after coming out of a religion as consuming as Mormonism. There were times I was still angered by the deception, plus I was also licking my wounds from the pain of rejection. But I also knew that when one is in that transitory state from religion to the great unknown, it is the absolute worst time for tug-of-war pulls coming from both sides of the fence. Personally, what I needed most was some validation that I was going to be okay. I needed comfort to get through the grief of divorcing myself from the people I once called my church family, and needed help deprogramming and recovering from a very deeply ingrained indoctrination.

It's not that Christians or Mormons are not well–versed in their holy books, nor should they feel compelled to be apologetics experts. People convert and leave religions and denominations for any myriad of reasons. Most of the time, converts have been invited by friends or family to attend church activities or events. I've attended some warm, loving, strong, dedicated Christian churches—communities that would put many LDS wards or stakes to shame. I've felt much more inspired and happy coming out of one single Christian service that had awesome, energetic worship and praise music than I ever spent in all my years in LDS music. At the same time, I remember the great times I had growing up in the Primary program as a child, and as an LDS youth. The activities, dances, trips, the various rites of passages through the Young Women's program, whereas some denominations of Christianity forbade dancing at all or didn't have enough teenagers to even have a youth program. I liked and have been a part of several Christian and LDS programs. Culturally speaking, I've had very few regrets being a part of both religions.

Both sides have some great qualities. Both have wonderful communities of people. But both sides also have some serious misconceptions about the other, and both are seriously afflicted with pride and hypocrisy. Both sides believe they lack nothing and believe they're righteous and true in every way, shape and form. But to tell the absolute truth, since the days of Christ Himself, *nothing* in the world's history has worked in bringing people together in the manner He admonished. Christianity hasn't; Mormonism hasn't; Islam hasn't; Buddhism hasn't; Catholicism hasn't. *No* religion has—in fact, there has only been more antipathy, confusion, and deeper division than ever existed before.

Despite this, I have come to believe that there is common ground that can be walked, not only for mainstream Christianity and Mormonism, but all religions of the world. So the questions should not be about conversion *to* or abandonment *from*. Rather, the questions should be:

> Where are the common grounds we can all walk together in *faith*, regardless of the vast amount of systematic beliefs and traditions?
>
> How can we change our attitudes, turn the clock of time towards a better day, and get out of the ruts of the same obvious bad road?

Where is the peace? It has to be found somewhere in this world, somewhere in history. I happen to believe it is found in Jesus Christ. If Jesus Christ could be what Mormonism and Christianity have in common, then the answer to the dilemma has become simple: bring both Mormons and Christians, as well as the rest of the world, out of religion and bring them to Jesus Christ.

And that is where we begin.

Mormons and Christians in Transition

First, it would help if we all approached the words of Jesus Christ anew, as if we were reading the Gospels for the *very first time*. No scripture cross-references, no personal interpretations or other translations; no speaking in tongues, no other holy books, no "restored gospel," no reciting belief statements, no translation hang-ups, no Bible study supplements. No Old Testament, no New Testament. *Just* the Gospels. *Just* the words of Christ. Reading His words for what they are, recognizing Him for who He is, and remembering Him for what He did. I feel this is exactly what needs to happen—as if Christ were plopped right in the middle of our lives today and we took His word and only His word for truth: taking the miracles, parables and teachings of His ministry and applying them to our lives, here and now. Not two thousand years ago—today. Because really, if Christ were to come back and look at Christianity, would He be pleased at the faithfulness to His teachings, or disappointed at how it has evolved into various denominational sects of confusion and complexity? Would Jesus be a card-carrying member of the LDS Church? Should both sides be more ashamed of themselves rather than trying to convince each other of their own righteousness? Does today's mainstream Christianity even remotely resemble anything Christ had taught?

I can tell you the answer to that question right now: *absolutely not*. Which is exactly why we are in the state we're in today. Humanity has gone through many changes and evolvements through the centuries; some may even call that progress. But the truth is, very little has changed regarding our attitudes about God since Jesus left the world and the "powers that be" in charge of the Christianity's future. We haven't honored "God in the flesh;" we've ignored God and listened to others, to ourselves. We haven't included God in our lives, much less God's only *Son*. In fact, many deny God's very existence. The Wonderful Counselor has not become our Rock of Ages; we use our own rocks to stone each other with. The Mighty God's teachings are not written upon our hearts; we've created our *own* belief systems, distorting and twisting the truth that is supposed to set us free, locking ourselves into a prison of our own ideologies, interpretations, revelations and justifications. The Everlasting Father has been reduced down into a box of organized, systematic belief statements, an icon, a ritual, a marketing campaign, slogan or bumper sticker. We close our minds, indignant towards those who try to tell us the world is round, when "everyone knows it's flat." Denial has become another cancer of truth.

We haven't come together as peacemakers under the wings of the Prince of Peace; we segregate, discriminate, argue, wage war and destroy. We knowingly deceive. We get in each other's faces, confront and provoke. Instead of forgiveness, we want revenge disguised as justice. We haven't loved our neighbors or our enemies; we have become our *own worst enemies*. We are just as idolatrous as ever before—the golden calves we've created far outweigh any that Israel could have ever conceived or forged—and we market them without conscience! We aren't really followers of Christ, we merely *act* like we are—hypocritically praying on the street corners "to be seen of men," sitting in the high seats of the synagogues, churches, cathedrals, temples, tabernacles, testifying and praying "*Lord, Lord . . .* "

> Not everyone that saith unto me, Lord, Lord, shall enter into the kingdom of heaven;
> but he that doeth the will of my Father which is in heaven.

> Many will say to me in that day, Lord, Lord, have we not prophesied in thy name? and in thy name have cast out devils? and in thy name done many wonderful works?
>
> And then will I profess unto them,
> I never knew you: depart from me, ye that work iniquity.
> Matthew 7: 21–24

Ouch. Pretty strong words. Would Christ even recognize those who are claiming to be Christians, those claiming to know Him? Humanity—who has crucified Jesus over and over again through the centuries—in claiming discipleship has ironically found itself, again, in desperate need of a Savior.

We have become our own anti-Christ.

Forgive Us Our Trespasses

Well, folks—if we are to get a fresh new start with a common grounds approach, we obviously need to, at the very least, take some brief, embarrassing peeks at where we've been. If we are to change the world, we need to clearly understand the mistakes made so we don't keep repeating them. Sounds simple enough, right? Remember, we've ignored Christ's words for so long that this actually may be a pretty tough exercise, especially when we have people in powerful leadership positions that still refuse to learn from our history lessons. Fortunately, I've found chapters 23 and 24 of the Gospel of Matthew a great place to start in order to fill in those centuries-old gaps of ignorance. We need to *remember what we've learned.*

It is time—past time, if you ask me!

The Woes of Hypocrisy

Matthew 23 is Jesus' Woes of the Pharisees. We don't even need to single out that particular sect of Judaic authority to realize that hypocrisy is a global problem that all religions have been plagued with. Several times I've witnessed first-hand the "do what we say and not as we do" excuse rampant in both Mormonism's and Christianity's leadership. Jesus prophetically strikes against such in Matthew's chapter 23.

> Everything they do is done for men to see.
> They make their phylacteries wide,
> and their tassels long . . .

For many religions, much of it seems to be all about image. Do we look good? Do we at least have the appearance of good? Nothing says special like a particular dress code. Those handsome young nineteen-year-old Mormon missionaries with their white shirts, ties and black nametags look quite dapper from haircut to shined shoes. But Mormons aren't the only ones who believe that dressing up is the way to go. There are many religions that have succumbed to a specific code of dress. However, all should beware that pride sets in when one starts excluding or rejecting people, or looking down their noses at something as inconsequential as fashion or lack thereof. Whether in jeans and a t-shirt, or a three-piece suit—Jesus could care less about fashion. Would Jesus like to see the Pope all decked out and adorned in decorative robes trimmed in gold, or the LDS General Authorities clad in three-piece suits and ties? Would Jesus rather see us for who we appear to be . . . or for who we really are?

> And why take ye thought for raiment?
> Consider the lilies of the field, how they grow;
> they toil not, neither do they spin:
> And yet I say unto you, That even Solomon in all his
> glory was not arrayed like one of these . . .
>
> . . . therefore, take no thought, saying,
> What shall we eat? Or, What shall we drink?
> Or, Wherewithal shall we be clothed?
> Matthew 6: 28–31

I'm not going to get into details about religious apparel, whether worn on the outside or underneath. My objective is certainly not to offend, but to have us stop and think about some of the trivial things that clutter up soul space and shifts our focus away from those spiritual garage sales we're entertaining!

> They love the place of honor at banquets, and
> the most important seats in the synagogues.

For every time I saw the bishop seated in the front of the chapel flanked by counselors, looking down over the congregation, this is actually a woe quite disturbing for me to think about. When I dutifully watched the LDS Church's Semi-Annual General Conference, the General Authorities were always seated in the "important seats" in the front for the world to see. When I met Gordon B. Hinckley at BYU, he and his entourage, including body guards and security, were all well-dressed, arriving in black shiny cars and treated like royalty. There are both Mormon *and* Christian figureheads alike who have fallen into the trap of celebrity and fame. But what's really scary to think about is that tithing money—from both the terribly rich and the terribly poor—is funding it all. So you have a poor family in a third world country barely scraping by trying to pay a ten percent tithe on nearly nothing *so some suits can have a limo ride to their next gig*? Both they and the people who place those leaders on such pedestals are at great fault in perpetuating pride disguised as meekness. I say to the poor: *Please, keep that money and buy food for your hungry families!*

> . . . they love to be greeted in the marketplaces,
> and to have men call them "Rabbi" . . .

Ah, titles of honor! Pope. Prophet. President. Master. Buddha. Enlightened One. Father. Reverend. Good master. Titles about as useful as a dress code. I will never forget the time our LDS ward had a visiting General Authority for a priesthood meeting before a Stake Conference. My then husband told me that he had to use the restroom before the meeting, and scratched his head as he read a sign taped on the door: "General Authorities Only". He looked over to the women's bathroom where the sign had been changed to "Men." Wow. GA's can't pee in the same room with others? I'm sorry, but this borders on ridiculousness—or achieves it—when we think someone else's urine or feces is holier than ours! Blessed urinals aside, how exciting would it be for a devout Mormon to see and shake hands with a General Authority in their local grocery store? What about an opportunity for a devout Christian to meet Billy Graham personally at their place of worship? Or watch the Pope in his royal garb wave his hands of blessing over your section of the thronging crowd?

I know this may seem a little direct. Perhaps you've even been offended. Maybe you think there's nothing wrong with dressing up, or esteeming those with religious authority. But I ask that you not be upset, but more convicted in your hearts, for as you read on through Jesus' Woes listed in Matthew 23, I'd say I've been pretty mild in comparison. Read on:

Shutting the door on you (verse 13): I don't know if it's ego that comes into play here, but there has been a prideful, worldly attitude perpetuated for ages now that knowledge is given and possessed only by a privileged few. As if God has an exclusive membership of elites that He imparts His will to. I'll talk a little more about "God's Chosen People Syndrome" later on in this chapter.

Praying (or preying) upon the poor (verse 14): Forgive the play on words, but this, I believe, is a woeful hypocrisy that I've already expounded upon. The rich and powerful are made richer, while the poor are kept poor. But in order to make this hypocrisy unapparent, the leaders lend long prayers to the poor so that it makes them *appear* as if they care. Truth is, they're too busy with their own packed agendas and schedules to really care. Okay, giving them the benefit of the doubt, let's say that maybe they do care. But their prayers are useless if *nothing changes*. And obviously, nothing has changed—the homeless and the poor continue to be among us.

Conversion (verse 15): This one really struck home to me, considering the LDS Church's comprehensive missionary efforts. It's really quite staggering to think about how many millions of dollars are budgeted on marketing campaigns and propaganda for religions to sell their wares to potential converts, when again, the money could be better spent buying food, clothing and housing for the poor. I mean, c'mon—did Joseph Smith really think he could do better with the fictitious Book of Mormon than Jesus' Beatitudes or the Sermon on the Mount? The good news of Jesus Christ doesn't need any convincing, selling, marketing, or additional testaments. Believe me, grace sells itself!

Blind guides (verse 16). This woe is a little complex upon the first read-through, but I generally understand it as "fools making the rules." The thing I find most interesting is that Jesus addresses them: *"Woe to you, blind guides!"* Now there's a visual—no pun intended. Could you imagine relying upon a blind guide to lead you down a narrow cliff road filled with various dangers in the path? Of course not. So why would we allow a blind guide to tell us what to do, or lead us down our own spiritual paths of life's inevitable twists, turns, and perils?

Neglecting goodness for the sake of "the rules" (verse 23). The parable of the Good Samaritan is a great illustration of how leaders use excuses to avoid charitable acts of kindness and mercy for the sake of the rules. This woe also displays how one can claim to charitably give, but pass by the other side and completely miss the mark by not giving what is obviously needed *more*—justice, mercy, faithfulness. But most of all, *love*. If someone is hungry and needs food, would you give them flowers instead? If someone needs shelter, would you impart a lesson from a church magazine? If someone needs clothing, would you give him a barrel? Money, and you clip a coupon for them? You get the picture. Do good where the good is really needed.

Keeping up appearances (verses 24–28): These two deal with façades—looking good on the outside, but the inside is "full of hypocrisy and wickedness." Like actors on a stage, façades have both fooled and destroyed people. They nearly destroyed me. I had that smile pasted on my face so many times, acting like the perfect Molly Mormon on the outside when the truth was that my life was an absolute wreck. It's truly is amazing, the lengths many religions will go to in order to sell people on Trojan horse type organizations and programs. But what is even more amazing are the lengths that many members of a religion will go to in order to sell it—even if it means living a lie to gain one convert or follower.

Being honest with ourselves (verses 29–32). This is one has prophetic impact, as Jesus cuts to the very heart with the *"I wouldn't have done that"* hypocrisy. This one is taught to little children on the playground—those who sit back and watch a group of bullies beating someone up. Other kids may not have directly participated, but they witnessed the event and didn't do anything about it—either out of fear of being beaten up themselves, or becoming unpopular with the majority that felt the beating was justified. Today, could we say, *"If I had lived back then, I wouldn't have participated in the crucifixion of Christ"*? Hopefully, yes. Historically speaking? No.

The Cure for Hypocrisy

Hypocrisy can be a tough thing to overcome, but remember, not impossible. Jesus gives us the cure for the disease of hypocrisy: humility.

> "But you are not to be called Rabbi, for you have only one Master, and you are all brothers. And do not call anyone on earth "father," for you have one Father and He is in heaven.
> Nor are you to be called "teacher," for you have one Teacher, the Christ.
> The greatest among you will be your servant.

For whoever exalts himself will be humbled,
and whoever humbles himself will be exalted.
(Matthew 23: 8–12)

Taking Heed: Matthew 24

Chapter 24 contains Jesus' End of Days prophecies. I find it ironic that Jesus Christ, the Prince of Peace foretells anything *but* peace. It is that same irony that causes me to believe that the anti-Christ, be it a literal or figurative symbol of Christ's antithesis, is something that has been forged and refined over a long period of time. I am confident that Christianity today is nothing like Jesus had taught, and nor would He, regardless of any so-called renaissances, reformations or restorations endorse what has now evolved. Albeit something sure took off like wildfire, whatever it was certainly didn't include the Jesus Christ who implored us to love one another. Christianity is a mess, with religions such as Mormonism not making it any better, and it will all become an unmanageable beast that will destroy humankind if it is not recognized and defeated now.

I won't expound upon the whole chapter of Matthew 24, though I do highly recommend you read it in its entirety, but the elements that impact me the most from Christ's prophecies are the following (bold added):

> Take heed that no man deceive you.
> For many shall come in my name, saying, I am Christ;
> and shall deceive many.
> Matthew 24: 4–5

...And many false prophets shall rise, and shall deceive many.
And because iniquity shall abound, the love of many shall wax cold
Matthew 24: 11–12

...Then if any man shall say unto you, Lo, here is Christ, or there; believe it not.
For there shall arise false Christs and false prophets, and shall shew great signs and wonders; insomuch that, if it were possible, they shall deceive the very elect.

Behold, I have told you before.

Wherefore if they shall say unto you, Behold, he is in the desert; **go not forth**:
behold, he is in the secret chambers; **believe it not**.

For as the lightning cometh out of the east, and shineth even unto the west;
so shall also the coming of the Son of man be.

For wheresoever the carcass is,
there will the eagles be gathered together.
Matthew 24: 23–28

Wow. Where to begin or even do justice in commenting on such a vivid representation of what has actually happened in human history! I find it interesting that Jesus uses the word "many." If there were any danger signs in these passages, we should be paying attention to that word in particular. If there be common grounds connections among us, it would be that not just a few of us have been deceived—many of us have been deceived. Not only that, we've been convinced to believe things that we shouldn't. Like the story of *The Emperor's New Clothes,* we start seeing and believing things that aren't really true, but it sounds so convincing that we end up believing that they must be true. It's not an obvious trap, because so many things that religion tries to sell you really do seem to feel good and right. All religions are guilty of this trapping of souls, and Jesus is trying to help us avoid getting entangled in such feel-good marketing to the masses. Remember—if it seems to good to be true, it probably is. Take heed!

It is compelling, to say the least, that Jesus talks about false Christs and false prophets and what they will specifically say and do. He tells us not to believe it when they say, "here or there is Christ." He tells us that false Christs and prophets shall deceive "the very elect." It's a warning provided by Christ himself! But what have the historical patterns of the world shown? We ended up believing what He explicitly told us not to believe! This has happened countless times—from Paul's vision on the road to Damascus, to Mohammad claiming Allah's endowments in a cave, to Constantine claiming the same type of vision from a near-deathbed triggering the terrible, blood-filled Crusades, to Joseph Smith claiming the same thing in a grove of trees in upstate New York, to Hitler's terrible rise to power, to Jim Jones' and his followers to their graves, to Dave Koresh's Branch Dividians, to the Hale Boppers, to the many originators of the innumerable "here or there" claims made in history.

What does Jesus tell us to do when such claims are made? Believe it not! He even said that He's told us ahead of time, and we've still been suckers! Think we can finally get it? Those who claim to be those special, spiritual visionaries for your benefit should red flag you right away. Please, if someone tells you that they've had a vision or a revelation, and that you must do what they say, believe it not! The day has already come. We're in it, right here, right now. Don't believe it.

I had gone into the "secret chambers" of a few LDS temples. I seriously mean no disrespect, but if ever there were a gathering of eagles over carcasses, the temple ceremonies would be it. Now, if I had never experienced the goings on in LDS temples, my credibility in making such a statement would be questionable. But I have. The chants that I droned repeatedly, the rites and rituals I participated in and experienced first-hand truly were nothing but the contents of whitewashed tombs and a serious waste of time that could be spent actually going into the streets and doing some good among the poor and downtrodden. Some Mormons may disagree with me and claim they never felt closer to Jesus Christ than in the temple. That would be fine and dandy if it weren't the Mormon Jesus Christ—a false Christ—that you were feeling so close to.

Sorry to burst the bubbles of any future Mormon converts, but there is absolutely nothing special that goes on inside the Mormon temples. It is truly a house of mirrors. Don't go—you will not find the real Jesus in there. Besides, Jesus himself warned us ahead of time on that one, too: "behold, he is in the secret chambers; believe it not . . ."

> For nothing is secret, that shall not be made manifest; neither anything hid that shall not be known and come abroad.
> Luke 8:17

These things may be hard to hear, and may even invoke some pretty hard feelings, especially among our LDS comrades. Some of you may really struggle with what I've said. For example, I included Paul and his Damascus vision in the mix, not to discount his born again experience but to illustrate similarities between his and other visionary claims. Did Jesus' admonition include Paul's vision on his journey to Damascus? If Jesus said it, I would say, yes.

There are Christian denominations that have been whisked away in varying Pentecostal "gifts" that can make your average questioning Mormon think Christians are quite insane. These Christians don't realize that they're only validating the LDS claim that Christ's church was lost and in need of restoration. Also, Christians may not be aware of how similar the two visions of Paul and Joseph Smith are, except that Joseph Smith actually claimed to have seen Jesus Christ, not just hear him. However, the big difference between Paul's and Joseph's visions is that Paul had witnesses substantiating his born again experience on the way to Damascus, and ended up preaching the good news of Jesus Christ. He had gone through the needle's eye. Joseph Smith, however, claimed he had a vision with no substantiating witnesses, ended up writing a fictional book and created an entire religion based upon a false Christ.

Jesus also told us that His second coming would be as obvious to the entire world *"as the lightning cometh out of the east, and shineth even unto the west."* But Joseph Smith claimed that Jesus has come to the earth already, appeared to him in a grove of trees in a private vision with instructions to start a "restored church." Jesus? Promoting religion when He had warned about the hypocrisies of such in Matthew 23? Jesus came 2000 years ago to take us out of the boxes of religion and set us free—not to create more boxes to package God in.

So what or who do we believe? How are we to know the truth? In a world like ours, it is very difficult. Religion taints our pure, child-like faith by playing off of our belief. This is why Jesus wants us to simplify our spiritual lives by asking us to believe in Him and Him alone—God in the flesh—and "believe not" the rest. Jesus knew the risks involved when He said things that the Jewish leaders didn't want to hear, but yet He still said them. And He didn't say that religion or any certain church was the way, the truth and the life. He said that He was.

I truly apologize; I don't want to hurt anyone's feelings when it comes to these things, but sometimes the truth does, in fact, hurt. What I'm trying to do is convey, perhaps for the very first time for many of you, the reality of the world today. Sure, many religions and denominations may have a lot to lose by the simple words of Christ. But it doesn't diminish the compelling truth that Jesus' words have been ignored for two millennia.

> And ye shall hear of **wars and rumours of wars**:
> see that ye be not troubled: for all these things must come to pass, but the end is not yet.
> Matthew 24:6

Iniquity abounding. The love of many waxing cold. Wars and rumors of wars, with militias and armies increasing. Definitely prophecies already fulfilled! The world has become soulless, greedy, and cruel. How difficult it is to not be troubled in a world like ours today. How can these types of powerfully evolved patterns of hate and revenge be stopped? How can we act and react with love instead of spite, hate and revenge? How can we look at each other as brothers and sisters, instead of continuing the cruel, discriminating labels that separate us? How can we quit the spread of gossip, hypocrisy, misunderstandings and lies? How can we begin to grow together, instead separating ourselves from each other? Most of all, how can we get those who we've ushered into those cushy seats of leadership of religion and politics to do the same? It hasn't happened yet. Is such a feat possible to accomplish?

For those who want to come together on common grounds, it is imperative that we stop investing in the words of those who perpetuate such division and make deceptive claims. The "Age of

Religion" must come to an end. Don't believe those who claim to have seen Christ, whether in a grove of trees or elsewhere. Don't participate in or perpetuate the hypocrisies of religious hierarchies. Don't follow the crowds down the broad, wide paths of destruction, emptiness and death. Ignore them, knowing that such people exist, knowing that "these things must come to pass." The common grounds approach would be for all of us to live a life of love, compassion and forgiveness. Instead of bringing bad news, bring good news to the world *by actually doing good.* Go down a new road of paved with hope, instead of going down the same old deeply rutted one of trouble and despair. Love must be the pulling force, with understanding and forgiveness escorting us out of the ruts of hypocrisy and the prisons of pride. Our actions and reactions must be spurred by love and compassion, rather than offense and hate.

> Enter ye in at the strait gate: for wide is the gate, and broad is the way that leadeth to destruction, and **many** there be which go in thereat:
>
> Because strait is the gate, and narrow is the way which leadeth unto life, and **few** there be that find it.
> Matthew 7:13–14, bold added

Looking at the past and present timeline of events, which do you think is the greater challenge: Going where *many* go—or where only a few go? Be a part of some huge religion or church, or simply follow Jesus? These days it may be hard to tell, but believe me, the needle's eye is a pretty narrow path to take us out of our comfortable little bubbles.

" . . . and come, take up thy cross and follow me."

Jesus Christ: God Cannot be Destroyed

The events surrounding the birth of Christ have given meaning to the holiday of Christmas. If angels sang to shepherds, if Mary was a divine mother, if wise men acknowledged the Messiah's arrival and bore gifts, then what an exciting birthday to celebrate! Whether or not you believe these things happened, Christ came into the world as a vulnerable infant, just like all of us. The simple belief? The Intangible became tangible.

Likewise, the events surrounding His death have given meaning to the holiday of Easter—the pain of Gethsemane, the crucifixion at Golgotha, the stone rolled away, breakfast on the beach with His disciples, His ascension into the heavens. Whether or not you believe these things happened, Christ experienced the pain of physical death, just like all of us. The simple belief? The tangible became Intangible once again.

That's it. Yes, it's that simple. The Good News of Jesus Christ is simply this: God cannot be destroyed. God, the Creator, the Supreme Force of all that is and ever will be, did not and never will die. If so, everything in the universe would immediately cease to exist. But fortunately for us, an infinite God who has control of time, including the dimensions of life and death, the seen and unseen, the known and unknown, came to show and prove it to us. Humankind from the beginning has looked to the skies of time and space, wondering about that something greater than ourselves. So if there were just one icon of belief to be had, just one sign to us that God is mindful of creation and life, could there be a better one than that very infinite Creator experiencing a finite condition out of love for His creations? If so, would that not be a significant event? And why would God do that?

A beautiful depiction to answer that question would be that of a parent getting down on the floor with their child, entering their world, looking into their child's eyes, playing with their toys, laughing with them, communicating with them and loving them. Likewise, God actually came into our dimension, our world, to understand His created, see us at eye level, laugh with us, cry with us, talk with us, teach us, break bread with us, feel our pains, our joys—to love us for who we are, right where we are. That's why He did it: love.

Jesus performed great miracles in order to be believed, not discounted. Again, did they really happen? Did He really do all of those things? I don't know. Maybe. I wasn't there; neither were you. But I'll tell you this much: today, word would spread like wildfire if we knew of a man "with healing in His wings," who turned water into wine, walked on water, caused the blind to see, the lame to throw their wheelchairs and crutches away, raised a man who had been dead for three days, and calmed a tumultuous storm. The press would be all over a man who fed 5000 people on a little bread and fish. If Jesus' past miracles would cause you to believe in Him, would you? And if just the present, every day miracles of the life around you caused you to believe, would you? Would my eye-opening, born again experience through the needle's eye convince you? Would reading the Gospels persuade you? Could you accept an unexplainable, intangible, powerful God's miracles and motives of unconditional love, with the simple choice being belief or unbelief in Him?

I like to think of miracles as being metaphysical confirmations or answers to prayers, whether in general or personally. If Christ specifically came to you and immediately healed you of your disease or ailment, as He did me, would you believe? Even if He didn't heal you, could you understand the purpose of your life and be His instrument, as the blind man in John 9 was for me? That's a lot of years to live in darkness, or be plagued with disease or blindness. Could you understand God's will through the purpose of your own life in helping others in an ignorant, lost world remember what we've learned?

Would you have believed that the best wine you ever tasted in your life at your friend's wedding was previously just pots of tap water? Could you sleep like a baby in a cradle while being tossed around in a storm-rocked boat? If you were told that mud made of dirt and the saliva would cure your blindness, would you allow Him to rub that stuff right on those faded peepers? If you were out in a boat and saw Jesus walking on the water towards you, waving *"Hey folks, it's just me, don't be afraid . . ."*

I'm sure you catch my drift. It seems there were two camps in Jesus' time—those who believed and witnessed or personally experienced miracles in their lives, and those who did not believe and discounted the miracles. Even today, those who are skeptical about things as supernatural as miracles may feel they have more to gain by dismissing them as impossible, while those who step out in faith and have nothing to lose are much more open to the possible. Ironically, when that happens, the miracles happen. The Pharisees discounted the miracle that happened to the blind man in John 9, just as quite a few Mormons discounted the miracle of my being born again in Jesus Christ. They couldn't believe that there could possibly be something better than what Mormonism had to offer. Disbelief can often cause a worse blindness:

> "For judgment I am come into this world, that they which see not might see; and they which see might be made blind.
> And some of the Pharisees which were with him heard

> these words, and said unto him, Are we blind also?
> Jesus said unto them, If ye were blind, ye should have no sin:
> But now ye say, We see; therefore your sin remaineth.
> John 9: 39–41

Whether believer or unbeliever, the existence of everything in this universe comes down to one thing: purpose. The miracles of Christ that have been recorded in the Gospel accounts may only be a fraction of all the miracles He did in His lifetime, but their purpose is clear: to help us believe. Not to believe in useless, trivial things, or made up mythological stories that confuse us, but to help us believe in the things that truly matter to us as human beings. And even though we may not understand some things that happen, or cannot see the purpose, it does not mean there is none. There is purpose to pain and suffering just as much as there is for joy and health, with the answers to "why" questions often revealed through the passage of time. As finite beings, time is something that we have no control of. We know how our own through the eye of the needle journeys have or can change our lives as we look back at the tracks our own timelines have forged. I look back and see that my own journey is nothing less than a miracle. What if we looked back at the world's history, realized the purpose of everything that has happened, good and bad, and finally chose to make a miracle of good happen on a massive global scale? The entire planet—now spurred by love—to be born again through the needle's eye?

I personally believe we've all gone through quite enough hurt. A miracle like that would be most welcome right about now.

> Blessed are those who haven't seen, yet believe.
> John 20:29

Nothing kept Jesus from ultimately dying on a cross, so obviously He didn't do all those miracles for His own health and well-being. He did them so the world would *believe* in Him again—and for many of us, for the very first time!

Common Grounds: What To Do

So where do we begin? Do we implore forgiveness for our prodigal meanderings? Can we admit our weaknesses, vulnerabilities, mistakes and blunders? Can we start over, let go of the baggage and realize the purpose of past events? Can we finally let go of the hurt, the offenses, the horrors perpetrated along the paths of human history? Could the LDS church forgive me for breaking their temple covenants? Could I forgive them for deceiving me? Could the Jews forgive Hitler, the American Indians forgive the U.S. government for perpetrating genocidal massacres? Could the U.S. forgive Osama bin Laden? Could Osama bin Laden forgive us? Could the African American race forgive the chains of slavery? Could the KKK and white supremacists see other races with new healed eyes? Could all conflicts and divisions across this tired Earth cease? If the answer is no, the world will never change its current destructive course.

Has the response of war and violence worked in achieving peace among the nations? Has religion historically helped us or hurt us? If not, could we all truly forgive those who have trespassed against us? I ask everyone, everywhere: *Is forgiveness on such a monumental, global scale even possible?*

Pretty heavy stuff, but I can tell you that answer right now: absolutely. We can and should do it, and do it *immediately.* We should all just stop, right now—stop the world and shift into a paradigm of forgiveness and peace, shedding the burdens and baggage of conflict. Stop trying to destroy each other, bring down the walls that divide us, and see each other, eye to eye, for the first time in a world of beautiful colors. Let the blinders of racism, prejudice, pride, greed, hypocrisy and division fall from our eyes. How could something of that magnitude be possible to accomplish?

> With men this is impossible; but with
> God all things are possible.

Would meeting on common grounds require forgiveness? Maybe it will require some now; maybe some in varying degrees down the road. All in all, I believe we have much to learn from and about each other, so let's start down the road of the possible and begin anew. Wipe the slate clean with that spirit of forgiveness. Bring all of the scarlet letter-pinning, finger-pointing, judgmental gossip to a screeching halt. Free everyone from the chains of guilt, blame and regret, and truly find rest unto our souls. Gone is the "he said, she said" gossip. Gone are the labels of infidels, non-member, inactive, or gentile. Gone are the cancers that feed upon the truth. With God in the equation, our *common grounds* equation, all things are possible.

> Come unto me all ye that labor and are heavy laden,
> and I will give you rest.
> Take my yoke upon you, and learn of me.
> For I am meek and lowly of heart, and ye shall find rest
> unto your souls.
> Matthew 11:28–30

A Very Good Place To Start: Love

No matter which hand is extended first, the manner in which it should be done is how Jesus did it—with *love*. Premeditated offense and defense play no part; just setting a neutral tone can be difficult enough to achieve right out of the gate. Often, Christians approach Mormons as a heretical cult, and Mormons approach others as superior because of their "only true restored gospel," using the labels of non-member, even anti-Mormon to protect their fears of the unknown. Factions of Islam use the word "infidels". Denominations of Christianity, by their very existence, segregate themselves. This is absolutely ridiculous! Who knows how many times Christ the Rabbi was approached by members of the Sanhedrin with premeditated, carefully calculated schemes in order to trip Him up? It's time to wipe the slate clean. Setting aside all pride, egos, biases and preconceived agendas would do *all* religions well, for . . .

> There is none good but one, that is, God . . .

Compassionate Listening: Focus!

In order to get a true understanding of each other, we need to stop talking and listen. Jesus taught and healed with compassion and understanding when dealing with all kinds of people in all sorts of situations and dilemmas. The impact of the Sermon on the Mount couldn't have been so eloquently delivered if Jesus couldn't get a word in edgewise. Trivial worries did not occupy His mind—He wasn't thinking about what was for dinner that night when the Roman centurion approached Him to heal his servant, nor did He sit around wondering if He had enough time to feed five thousand people before the bus left for Capernaum, or whether His robe would be dry cleaned in time for His triumphal entry into Jerusalem.

Jesus moved with compassion. He was totally in the moment. His attention was focused upon the people, right where they were. He took advantage of those teaching moments. At least, that's the way it has been recorded for us in the Gospels. So if you desire to open a common grounds dialogue, do it with compassionate listening and focus on the people around you. Don't be formulating your next comment or try dominating air time. Be considerate; really, truly *listen*. Respect those around you and find equilibrium that will be a benefit, not a hindrance, to all.

It's Okay to Question

"When our leaders speak, the thinking has been done. When they propose a plan—it is God's Plan. When they point the way, there is no other which is safe. When they give directions, it should mark the end of controversy. God works in no other way. To think otherwise, without immediate repentance, may cost one his faith, may destroy his testimony, and leave him a stranger to the kingdom of God."
Improvement Era, June 1945 (LDS publication)

"How fortunate for governments that the people they administer don't think."
—Adolf Hitler

One of the things that I found extremely distressing as a Mormon in transition was the fear of verbalizing my doubts and disbeliefs regarding the religion. Not in an anti-Mormon way, but in a most sincere, seeker-motivated way. I actually did feel sorry that I didn't believe the Book of Mormon anymore, and that I was also having second thoughts about the Bible. At the same time I feared no one would ever understand my plight if I pretended that I *didn't* doubt or question the things I was sincerely having trouble with. It was a little scary to step out and pursue those answers after living in a *Pleasantville*-type world of so many absolutes for thirty years. But I didn't need to be testified to, I didn't need to be reprimanded or condescended, made to feel like a dummy, be told I'm a "stranger to the kingdom of God"—nor did I need to feel guilty or compelled to repent about taking on such a search for answers to my questions. All I really needed was to feel free to ask questions that I needed to in my search for the truth, without the suppression of religious fear and guilt. At the same time, my curiosity was more peaked as to what would trigger such strong defensive declarations, so-called revelations, or reactions by religious leadership—such as "the thinking has been done"—if religions with doctrines comprised of black, white and a few shades of gray had nothing to hide.

Free Agency: What it Really Is

It is okay to ask questions, even the most difficult ones. The doors of free agency should be free to swing wide open, as Jesus said, "And ye shall know the truth, and the truth will set you *free,*" (John 8: 32, italics added). The burdens of any previous guilt should be lifted in that very statement alone. It's okay to say you don't believe something if you don't. It's okay to have feelings of doubt. What if Galileo hadn't the courage to claim his heliocentric ideas to the world? What if the Wright Brothers actually believed they were crazy for trying to invent something that would fly? But also, what if a majority of Germans had stepped up to the plate earlier and had the courage to say, "Something about this Hitler fellow just isn't right." What if more God-fearing people than government-fearing people stood up for the indigenous tribes of America or the black slaves, and had the timeliness and courage to say, "Something about what we're doing to these people just isn't right." If only there was less fear and more questioning of authority. If only there were more Rosa Parks in the world! Remember that last woe of hypocrisy? Do we sit just sit back and watch as injustice and deception rage on and consume the world? Or do we take the opportunities and associated risks to change the world?

Much of it may have to do with apathy and ignorance, or maybe a little of both. Apathy in that most people don't want to rock the boat, uneasily accepting the status quo. Ignorance in that many don't know or care what they believe, because the religion's culture and lifestyle is the reason they stay. I've spoken with Mormons who have told me they don't worry about all that doctrinal stuff; they don't understand it or don't want to get into it. "That's for the leaders to do," they say. They may even take pride in the fact that they don't have to think, relying on the "continuing revelation" of the prophet and General Authorities of the church, bearing their testimonies that they "know the church is true." But unfortunately, they don't "know" it. Why? Because I, like generations of Mormons before me, had been programmed to drone the same type of testimony! So everyone's testimonies start sounding the same—a theme with a few variations that compromises both individuality and genuineness.

The problem wasn't that the Mormon Church didn't have answers to my questions. They just weren't the right answers! The problem is, LDS answers are tailored to polarize Mormons to stay in the religion, even if those answers, no matter how sincere, fly directly in the face of reality, common sense, fact or reason. For me, most of the answers I was given resulted in pattern of circular logic, which is why I call Mormonism a doctrinal labyrinth. God gave me a brain, so I used it, and rather than continuing to look to the Mormon Church, I searched for the answers myself. Sure, it may have rocked the boat or comfort zones of those within the Mormon bubble—obviously enough to reject me—but as I said before, I would have rather known the truth and be set free, than be content to ignorantly live a lie and remain in a cage with "continuing revelation" bones being tossed to me now and then.

People are becoming more and more vocal, questioning issues that pertain to and concern them. It's okay to do this. Even if you are in a situation where you cannot vocalize it, it's okay to think it and be honest with yourself when things just don't seem right. So think. Ask. Seek. Knock. One idea can change the world. It all starts with a question.

Breaking the Ice: Finding Familiar Grounds

Let's talk. If there's anything I know about the cultures of both Mormons *and* Christians, it's that everyone likes a good get-together. And if you make a mean apple pie or chocolate cake, that's points right there! I personally love to barbecue. Though perfect strangers, it seems that Jehovah Witnesses, Mormon missionaries and vacuum salespersons are often invited right into potential converts' homes, where they seem to be most comfortable. If you are so inclined, open up your home for a potluck, or reserve a table at a favorite or agreed-upon restaurant or coffee shop that can accommodate a group. And even though Mormons don't drink coffee, there are other menu items that are kosher. Public places can, by default, act as deterrents of potential heated discussions, debates, or situations that could go awry. It's always good to have a drink in hand, anyway, if but used as nothing but a prop to make one feel comfortable. Breaking bread with each other is a tradition in many cultures. Do it. Don't get together as Mormons or Christians—forget the labels and let's get together as friends!

If you must meet at a church, I would avoid consistently meeting at any one particular church, so mix it up a little. What you're looking for is a laid-back environment conducive to objectivity and open discussion—not argument and division, which would defeat the common grounds purpose from the get-go. Most would not have a problem meeting in perhaps a recreational building separate from the main church, but still others may be uncomfortable, so be sensitive in the planning of the environment. Strangers can become friends when the surroundings are favorable for everyone. Nicodemus asked Jesus to come chat with him at night, where he could get a moment without being hammered by the burdens and requirements of his legalistic religion and those who might "talk." Remember, it's okay!

It is good to meet face to face, in a group. That way you know it's real and you are not alone. I would shy away from Internet discussion or chat groups. I know the Internet can be a great tool for many things, but also remember that it's not only a virtual world, it provides a façade for wolves in sheep's clothing to infiltrate an otherwise productive discussion. I used to go into Internet chat rooms where I thought those participating in discussion-turned-arguments were actually helping me in my recovery and transition from Mormonism, only to discover they were either Mormons trying to convert me back, or Christians who wanted to point out doctrinal and theological differences. With both well meaning Mormons and Christians unable to understand each other, the discussion always ended up becoming a destructive tug of war, leaving me in the middle and more frustrated than convinced that either side had my best interests at heart. Know when to pull back the reins for the sake of respect and peace.

Translations/Versions. The reason I'm using the King James Version for my scriptural references is because I know it is the only accepted version Mormons use. Granted, the Old English version can be a little problematic for Christians who may be used to the plain language of the New International Version or New Living Translation or other translations. It would just be easier for Christians to concede their translation preferences for harmony's sake.

In turn, the Mormons must forfeit their Joseph Smith Translation Bible references, the Book of Mormon, Doctrine & Covenants and Pearl of Great Price. The Gospels are the Gospels, and I think no Mormon or Christian in their right mind would question that the very words of Jesus Christ supercedes all, regardless of what the translation is. If it does bother you, perhaps you have a few more knick-knacks to get rid of in that spiritual garage sale!

Prayer. I've also noticed that the manner in which one prays can seem a little strange to some. Some prayers sound almost recited and formal, some casual and to the point, others a little more personal and intimate. Be accepting and considerate as to how people pray—I can also safely suggest the way of prayer as taught by Jesus Christ Himself: The Lord's Prayer. Anyone can either recite it verbatim from Matthew 6: 9–12, or use it as a guide. In any event, prayer is the common grounds connection that invites God into the mix, so it's only logical that discussions should begin with a prayer in order to set a tone of peace and neutrality. *Note: if your tendencies seem to be leaning toward atheism or agnosticism, which can often happen to a Mormon in transition—get over it for a while and humor everyone.*

The Denomination Abomination

If Christians everywhere are a part of the body of Christ, then why is there still such division and strife among us? Why so many denominational differences separating us? Why are we still finding the love your neighbor part of Christ's teachings difficult? And what part of love do we not understand?

Christians may be unaware that these various divisions and denominations are what actually started the Mormon religion. Joseph Smith said that he was so confused about which church to join that he claimed that both Jesus and God (two separate beings—yes, that would be polytheism) appeared to him in a vision. According to his account, "I was answered that I must join none of them, for they were all wrong . . ." (Joseph Smith History 1:19)

I'm sure Christians would like to believe that denomination factor is just a matter of preference as to how they uniquely worship. But the truth is, many denominations have become entire religions unto themselves. Like factions of Islam, there are both militant and peaceful Christians, with varying degrees in between. There are even denominations of Mormonism, such as the Reorganized Church of Jesus Christ of Latter-Day Saints (RLDS). There are even cultish Christian denominations, some centering around a particular element of belief, such as speaking in tongues or faith healing.

Many religious opportunists throughout the centuries have split off to create their own religions. Mormonism is just one of many. The irony now is that the LDS church wants to be recognized as Christian, because they claim to believe in Jesus Christ like mainstream Christianity. But wouldn't that contradict Joseph Smith's claim that he was told by God that Christian sects were "all wrong" and "an abomination in his sight"?

Remember:

> ...Then if any man shall say unto you, Lo, here is Christ, or there; believe it not.
> For there shall arise false Christs and false prophets, and shall shew great signs and wonders
> insomuch that, if it were possible, they shall deceive the very elect.
> Matthew 24:23:24

One day I was conversing with my husband, David, about the content of this book, and we got on the subject of churches. I asked, "What if churches weren't anything more than just place where anyone could find peace in a world filled with tribulation? A place of refuge, where we could worship, pray, and sing without any fear or inhibitions? Where we could meet and greet, give and share? What if all the churches of the world just took down their signs that differentiated their various denominational titles or religious persuasions, and listed their information in the phone book under one title: Church. That was it. From the most ornately decorated spires of a cathedral, temple, synagogue or mosque, to the smallest little church with a neon sign that points down into the basement of a building in the middle of a city block in a run-down neighborhood—if *all* churches just opened their doors to the world, stripped of all titles and labels, everyone knowing that there was a place that opened its doors for *everyone* to be loved and accepted.

David simply said, "For me, church starts on Monday."

What a great answer! Church is a community of people coming together like a large family. It's not about the place; it's about the people. It's not about the where; it's about the who. And definitely all about the love.

GCP Syndrome: Getting Over Ourselves

A very crucial step in the common grounds journey is finding the cure for what I call GCP Syndrome, or God's Chosen People Syndrome. Every religious faction in the world—to some extent, whether small or great—has this debilitating, problem which prevents achieving the common grounds of peace and love. GCP Syndrome is a big cause of segregation, discrimination, denominationalism, hypocrisy and dissension. To a large extent, GCP Syndrome is what creates religion in the first place.

As referenced in the woes of hypocrisy mentioned earlier in this chapter, recognizing the need for hope and belonging in human beings, whether individually or collectively, often causes those would-be authoritarian leaders to take advantage of the unsuspecting—somehow effectively convincing people that they have an "in" with God more than anyone else. Israel claimed to be God's chosen people, and look what they did to their own Messiah. And even if Jews don't believe that Christ was their Messiah, how would they even recognize any sort of deliverer in an unchanged world filled with the same types of hypocrisies, greed and destruction that existed then as now?

Though every religion would like to believe they have the corner of the market on God, the truth is this: God hasn't chosen anyone.

No person, no religion, no special group of people, no cult, *no one*. So, newsflash for future religious opportunists: sorry for the bad news, but GCP Syndrome has had its day.

Of course, all should realize that the cure for GCP Syndrome was, is, and always has been God. So you could say that God actually *did* chose someone: Jesus Christ, His own self made flesh. So it's time for us all to not only get over ourselves, but to humble ourselves sufficiently in realizing that God, by choosing Himself, has chosen *everyone*!

> Neither shall they say, Lo here! or, lo there!
> for, behold, the kingdom of God is within you.
> Luke 17:21

The Components of Faith and Belief

As painful as it was to enter and go through the needle's eye, I was so relieved and joyful to have rid myself of so much baggage. I had the garage sale, did a *lot* of dump runs and came out the other side with such a clean spiritual house that I was *so ready* for simple! In a world of so much complexity, the simple beauty of Christ's teachings is most gratifying. After living a life filled with beliefs for over thirty years, could I have really given up so many of them just to have just *one* remaining? Absolutely.

> The kingdom of heaven is like unto a merchant man,
> seeking goodly pearls:
> Who, when he had found one pearl of great price,
> went and sold all that he had, and bought it.
> Matthew 13: 45

Selling "all that I had" and starting over on the other side of the needle was just the beginning. In my exhaustive studies of world religions, I had found that none had made good on promises. *Not one.* Vast amounts of ideologies, visions, revelations, idols, myths and legends, beliefs—yes, the Bible inclusive—had adulterated *simple faith.* History has shown us over and over that no belief system or religion has ever succeeded in accomplishing peace and love on a grand scale—that "change-the-world" type of action. Sure, attempts have been made; Christianity has even attempted it. There have been wonderful icons of peace and love throughout the centuries, but unfortunately, an overwhelming amount of failures have rendered these successes ineffectual. Evil, hate and greed have choked out the goodness until despair, hopelessness, anger, and vengeance takes hold of people's hearts. Bottom line, there is still no peace in the world because we ourselves, our neighborhoods, our cities, our countries, the entire world has acted and reacted to each other in the same old ways.

Filling the empty space in my soul where my former beliefs once were, I've found for myself that Christ truly does make good on His promise of " . . . *I will give you rest."* How simple and powerful are the concepts of faith and love! I finally figured out that I didn't need a belief system, a path or several paths of Enlightenment, temple attendance, nor any secret knowledge or the observances thereof to answer the question: *what good thing shall I do, that I may have eternal life?*

I only needed one.

> For God so loved the world that He gave His only begotten Son, that whosoever believeth in Him should not perish, but have everlasting life.
> For God sent not his Son into the world to condemn the world;

but that the world through Him might be saved."
John 3:16–17

Not many—just *one single belief* in Jesus Christ. The purpose? So that we should not fear death, but live forever as promised. The common grounds of faith have been pure in all of us from the day we were born. And no matter what generation of time we were raised in, that child-like faith has been sorely tainted by far more previous generations of belief and tradition, exchanging that intangible faith for man made tangible beliefs. Nevertheless, the innocence and purity of our faith in something greater than ourselves—God—is and always will be there. And the great thing is that Jesus Christ came, not to condemn us, but to save us.

From what? From who? This time around, I'd definitely say *from ourselves!*

I am not saying we have no need for belief. Faith alone can make us pretty green in a world of random chaos, and reality can be a tough teacher. Today's world dictates that society is not kind. Fear can and often has spurred those figurative security blankets of belief that religion is chock full of. One disaster can level life's playing field with tragic events, such as 9/11, Hurricane Katrina or the Indian Ocean Tsunami. Just that one belief in God in the person of Jesus Christ can also solidly anchor us with strength to see past the tragedies and injustices and look forward to His calming of the storms, both literal and figurative. A toddler learning to walk in a forest of grownup legs can feel overwhelmed, but after taking a few hard falls, finds the will and determination to get up and eventually *stay* up. The harsh realities of life can be overwhelming, but belief can give us hope not only in ourselves, but each other. What that belief is *in* makes all the difference.

When we see a newborn infant sleeping, we are amazed at not just the miracle of life, but at its reliance on something greater. The trust factor is certainly implicit in baby's environment and those who care for it. It wasn't until I was born again that I was able to experience that incredible peace of knowing that my faith was, is and would always be, from that day on, in an awesomely incomprehensible infinite God—bound by nothing, in control of everything, including my own timeline. No living in a bubble, no biospheres with religious boundaries, but a promised eternal life beyond anything I could comprehend—treasure in heaven.

My one *belief* would be in that God who came in the flesh to hang out with us for a little while, offering His peace, His grace, and ultimately, His very life to a very complicated, lost little planet called Earth, suspended in that infinite universe of time.

What greater gift is there than God Himself?

> For the Father himself loveth you, because ye have loved me, and have believed that I came out from God.
> I came forth from the Father, and am come into the world:
> again, I leave the world and go to the Father.
> His disciples said unto Him,
> Lo, now speakest thou plainly, and speakest no proverb.
> Now we are sure that thou knowest all things,
> and needest not that any man should ask thee:
> by this we believe thou camest forth from God.
> Jesus answered them, Do ye now believe?
> Behold, the hour cometh, yea, is now come, that ye shall be scattered, every man to his own, and shall leave me alone:
> and yet I am not alone, because the Father is with me.
> These things I have spoken unto you, that in me ye might have peace.

In the world ye shall have tribulation: but be of good cheer;
I have overcome the world."
John 16: 27–33

FIVE

UNORTHODOX CHRISTIANITY

If you've made it this far, hopefully you have given up—or have at least considered giving up—the artificiality of religion cluttered with gratuitous beliefs. If the truth has set you free, how great is that freedom! And if the truth has offended you, it's probably healthy for you to be feeling that kind of conviction right about now.

One may possibly feel like they have been left with a big empty hole after such a housecleaning, but *don't despair!* It's not an empty hole—it's just that your soul's been *cleaned out,* and it's a very different feeling, maybe one you've never felt before. You may feel vulnerable, disoriented, distrusting and doubtful of yourself and others. You may be too fearful to attempt your own ex-communication and persuaded to go back to the security your religion or former beliefs. All of these thoughts and feelings are perfectly normal for those who are transitioning into the great unknown.

For many, this fork in the road moment is a pivotal time that can be the beginning of a very exciting, fulfilling journey. For others, a bitter attitude can develop holding one back in regret, anger, and pain; suspending them in the past and disabling them from moving forward. Still others may be scared to death to even step out of the house. I experienced most all of these things while in the process of leaving Mormonism. When a life has been consumed by way too many beliefs, a life of faith can be quite difficult to recognize again, if not altogether lost.

There is none good but one, that is, God.

The Journey of Faith

Regardless of the path you choose, you will need time to learn how to basically walk in the world again with that childlike faith. *It is critical that you take that time.* You will need to begin to not only trust your Creator again, but also to trust yourself as the Created. Give yourself some credit—you are a beautiful, unique creation! Forget the labels and stereotypes; ignore the discriminations and cruelties of a clueless world and first just learn how to *be* and *exist*. Stop whatever it is that has added all the complexities to life and start synchronizing your mind, heart and soul, concentrating on you and you alone. Leave behind any regrets from the former life that weighed you down, and really begin to *live*. Don't let anyone tell you what to do, that you *have* to do this or that, or guilt you into going back to a cluttered up life. And even if your transitioning experience leaves you agnostic or atheistic, everyone on this planet *must live by faith.* Not one single human being or creature has control of life, death or time anymore than one could assume total control of gravity, the sun's rays, or rotation of the Earth. Time moves infinitely forward. So make this *your* time to be in harmony with the realities of the creations around you. You need this; God *is* good and you are His perfect creation. So at this point, you need to just strip away everything you've ever been taught to believe about yourself by others, and learn to just *be*.

> Be ye therefore perfect; even as your
> Father which is in heaven is perfect.

Enjoy the wonders of every day life. Listen to yourself breathe in and out. Make a date with a beautiful sunrise or sunset. Listen to the birds sing—find out where the bird is, and what color it is. Go for a brisk walk or a jog along a flower or tree-lined street—feel your heart beat inside your chest. Do a cartwheel and run around on the grass in a park or a field. Dance. Look at the stars at night. Look closely at a wild flower or the leaves of a tree with a magnifying glass. Hike up to an overlook with binoculars. Look up at the sky, or lie down on a blanket on some green grass in a park and watch the clouds float by. Browse around a farmer's market and buy some produce. Crank up and sing your favorite songs in commute traffic. Go out in the rain without an umbrella and stomp in the puddles. Make a crackling fire in the fireplace, and steep your favorite tea or a mug of soup. Smell and taste different foods or scents—pop popcorn, crush garlic, grind fresh coffee beans, go wine tasting. Go through the doors of a bakery and inhale! Try different ethnic foods and spices. Take up a talent that you hadn't done in a while, or learn a new craft or skill. *Realize that you live in a beautiful world filled with miracles, of which you are a part.*

Experience the daily lives of *others*. Go to the neonatal unit of a hospital and watch the newborn babies sleeping and crying—watch the nurses care for them. Walk into a homeless shelter or food bank with your sleeves rolled up, ready to pack food boxes, make sandwiches or serve soup. While you're there, sit down and have coffee with some of the homeless people—have them tell you their story. If you play the guitar or piano (and can carry a tune—this is very important!), go to a retirement or nursing home, or hospice unit and sing and play for the residents there. Visit the wing of cancer or AIDS patients. Sit and listen to a group of veterans share their annals of war—maybe even record or write them down and compile them into a book to share with your local community. Put a few dollars in the guitar case of a street musician. Take a bunch of flowers to a cemetery and put a few on the graves of soldiers, or place some on those that don't have any flowers on them. Spend a day as a volunteer with a group of disabled or class of Special Ed kids. Be a part time mentor or tutor for elementary school children. *Realize that there are miracles around you in the form of people just like you.*

Experience peace and rest in your *own* soul. Find moments to meditate and relax. Pray the way *you* want to pray to the God of the Universe—and if you've made the mistake of throwing the baby out with the bathwater by shedding the belief in God, now is the perfect time to restore that innocent, untainted faith in that something greater than yourself. Go out and look at the star-filled skies, like the generations of humans before you and try to grasp how small you really are in the grand scheme of things. Realize that *you* are part of these infinite dimensions of time and space, and that you have purpose.

Now, here may be a challenge. Call someone you may have offended in the past and ask for forgiveness. Maybe the person you need to forgive the most is yourself. Forgive others as well—even if those who have offended you may have not asked for forgiveness and their hearts still may be hardened towards you. *Realize that regardless of whether or not they've offended you, they are beautifully created, too.*

Sleep like a baby again . . . *you are still a miracle!* In the beginning of your timeline was . . . you! It is high time for the created to meet the Creator. And if, by being born again through the needle's eye, you feel you're ready for something a little more unorthodox, read on.

"And He Shall Be Called . . ."

Was Jesus really the blameless sacrifice that died for the sins of the entire world? How can we rely on what we're told about Him? What was written about this obscure man in human history? Some assert that He was a rebellious, militant Jew who wanted to stir up a little controversy. Some claim that He was Israel's Messiah. Yet others say He was a prophet who was wise and did a lot of good. But who *was* Jesus, and what were the crimes that ultimately got Him crucified?

As far as I know, from my own personal studies, Jesus did not break any Judaic Law except for one: blasphemy. He made himself equal to God. Remember that the traditional definition of God according to *Mosaic* Law was the element that condemned Christ. He had literally called Himself the equivalent of *Jehovah* (Yahweh, or the Lord God), which apparently can get you into a lot of trouble with Israel's legal bar and a good majority of Orthodox Jews. In fact, it was trouble worthy of death, according to their law.

It is no wonder that Pontius Pilate, adjudicator of Rome, washed his hands of the matter dealing with Jesus' sentence. You can't blame Pilate for not knowing what to do; Jesus had committed no crime according to Roman law, so the Pharisaical arguments presented that Jesus had broken the Mosaic Law by calling himself God, or the "King of the Jews" may have caused Pilate to think, "So what? Who cares?" Israel's law meant little to Pilate, and furthermore, must have appeared archaically petty in comparison to Rome's pragmatic democracy. Would it have gotten Jesus in the same amount of trouble had He claimed, "I am the Son of Zeus," or "I am the Son of Caesar?" Possibly—but most likely not. Besides being considered a little crazy and everyone getting a good chuckle out of it, the whole ordeal may have made for great public relations propaganda to place Jesus in the annals of Roman mythology, putting Him on par with Hercules or Perseus. In fact, some believe the story of Jesus *is* mythology, and that the Gospels just make for a great story—some great man who was a healer that performed some miracles and wonders, and was pretty smart and wise besides. Many even believe the concept or idea of Jesus Christ or world savior developed over time as folklore or a tall tale that has been capitalized upon throughout the centuries. In any event, according to what we do know, at the time of Jesus' crucifixion, claiming deity certainly wasn't deserving of a criminal's death and Pilate knew this.

But Jesus did not only make himself equal with the God of the Jews; he claimed to be the Son of the God of the *entire universe.* Would He have been in trouble, not just with the Jews, but elsewhere . . . like say in *today's* world? Again, probably not. If Jesus came into the world claiming deity in the same way He did two thousand years ago as a small-town carpenter, I'm going to take a wild guess that the world's reaction would probably be just as mixed today as it was then.

> " . . . he [Jesus] asked his disciples, saying,
> Whom do men say that I the Son of man am?
> And they said, Some [say that thou art] John the Baptist:
> some, Elias; and others, Jeremias, or one of the prophets.
> He saith unto them,
> But whom say ye that I am?"
> Matthew 16:13–15

If Jesus' claim to deity was believed by all—including those who accused Him of being Who He said—if everyone recognized Jesus Christ for who He truly was at the time He walked the earth, with everyone believing who He claimed to be and actually living as He had taught, the world's history would have taken a very different turn. Perhaps that desperately needed shift towards peace—the peace still sorely needed for the world today—would have happened.

But it didn't, and you know what the amazing thing is? Jesus knew it wouldn't. Otherwise, wouldn't He have prophesied a peachy keen future for us in Matthew 24? But obviously such unachieved utopia is not the question here. No, the question still hangs in the air today as it did two thousand years ago: *Do we believe Him?* Do we believe that He's telling us the truth when He says He is the Son of God? Is He *credible*? Are His miracles, parables and teachings trustworthy? Are they enough for us to believe in Him, or do we seek another?

> Then came the Jews around about him, and said unto him, How long dost thou make us to doubt? If thou be the Christ, tell us plainly.
>
> Jesus answered them, I told you, and you believed not: the works that I do in my Father's name, they bear witness of me.
>
> But ye believe not, because ye are not of my sheep, as I said unto you. My sheep hear my voice, and I know them, and they follow me:
>
> And I give unto them eternal life; and they shall never perish, neither shall any man pluck them out of my hand.

> My Father, which gave them me, is greater than all; and no man is able to pluck them out of my Father's hand.
> I and my Father are one.
> —John 10: 24–30

Back then these are words the Jews certainly did not want to hear. So what about now, today? Can we trust the Gospel accounts enough to quantify His word for ourselves, to fill our souls with peace and spiritual edification? In avoiding habitual patterns of fear, blindness, and ignorance, relying on the beliefs we've naïvely allowed to have authority over our lives, minds and hearts? Not only that, is what He's asked us to do as cited in the Gospels even doable in a world such as ours today?

Or do we even want to bother? Would ignorance be more bliss? Would we rather stick with believing the Koran and the teachings of Mohammad, Joseph Smith's vision and Book of Mormon, hang on each word of the Dahli Lama, walk down the paths of Scientology, or thumb through books by the latest spiritual guru on the best seller's list? Continue on in the traditional tracks of Judaism, or Zen's Eightfold Path? Would we all be just fine if we were devoid of all belief? Why believe anything at all—what's wrong with just living our lives the way we want to, without believing anything, including God?

And here's a loaded question for Christians: Could you forsake all you've ever been taught in mainstream Christianity from Genesis to Malachi, Acts to Revelations—to follow Jesus Christ *alone*? It's a straight, narrow path that *few* find.

I know it's a lot of questions stemming from one simple one. But they're important, straightforward, logical questions to consider. Because either we want to keep our stressed out souls cluttered up with junk we don't need, or we want peace and rest once and for all. Could we sell everything we have, shedding *all* the beliefs in the world, and take a chance for that *one simple belief* in Jesus Christ, like He offered the young rich man? For either Jesus offers the world something better than anything else, or He doesn't.

The Good News

Are you ready for some good news? The message of the Gospels—Matthew, Mark, Luke and John—is simply this: to proclaim that God—*Wonderful, Counselor, the Mighty God, the Everlasting Father, the Prince of Peace* (Isaiah 9:6)—is aware of us, loves us, and wanted to show us just how much by making a personal appearance.

So a mighty, everlasting God came as a very unorthodox Jew that broke some pretty deep-seeded traditions which made Him quite unpopular: eating with unwashed hands, breaking the traditions of the Sabbath on more than one occasion, associating with sinners, hanging out in leper colonies, having dinner with prostitutes and tax collectors, etc.

How tradition became law for the Sanhedrin to judge Jesus' actions is not so far beyond comprehension. Why? Because nothing has changed since then. We have evolved uninterrupted on that same haughty religious path that accused and sentenced Jesus. Those deep-seeded traditions still exist today, although now our blindness has brought us to the point where ALL religions, not just Judaism, have systematically overwhelmed our innate, simple faith—we, the wonderfully created, have evolved to a point where we couldn't recognize our own Creator. What distracted us?

It certainly is perplexing that God would choose to leave the throne of infinite time to be raised in Judaism, one of the most complex of world religions. And I thought Mormonism was complex. The world has raised this type of complexity to a whole new level of exhaustion by adding on even more things that burden us, and we've done this for centuries on end. In fact, the very Old Testament law, traditions and scriptures that condemned Jesus to death are still used today with religion, crucifying Him over and over again. It's time that cycle was broken.

The Bible

This brings us to a very controversial part of this book for today's Christians to consider—after all, Mormonism had its turn, so I feel it only fair!

As I mentioned before, no one was around when I was born again, when I came to know my Savior and was healed of my spiritual blindness. Yes, it is through the Gospel of John that I came to know Him, and John's account is in the Bible. But you need to understand that I am not a Bible-believing Christian—I am a Jesus-believing Christian. There is a difference.

With all the studies I did on Judaism, I really didn't care what was said in the Old Testament; *I'm not a Jew.* Those are their books. And with all the studies I did on early Christian history, I really didn't care about what Paul or any compilation of books from Acts on had to say; *I'm not a Catholic.* Those are their books. The Gospels, however, are the scribed accounts of Jesus Christ. Now, those books do something for me.

I've heard sermons where Old Testament scripture and Pauline epistles had been quoted more than Christ's own word; in fact, they had even taken precedence over them, many times rendering Jesus' very teachings ineffective. I've even heard entire Christian sermons and sat through numerous LDS Sacrament Meetings where the name of Jesus Christ wasn't even mentioned at all, except tagged on like an afterthought at the end of a prayer. Whose words are taking more precedence over "the Word made flesh?" When did categorically-decided canonized scripture become more important or better than the Good News of Jesus Christ?

Moses didn't convince me. Paul didn't convince me. Religion didn't convince me. Agnosticism and atheism didn't convince me. Joseph Smith's story and the Book of Mormon didn't convince me, and the Bible didn't convince me. Not one sermon from a pulpit convinced me. Could the books that we deem holy become idols that have distracted us away from what Christ actually did say, that we've focused way too much on what He *didn't* say?

Jesus set a child in the midst of His disciples as an example of what the kingdom of heaven was like. So what invaded our pure faith relationship with God? We haven't even practiced the very basics of what Jesus taught, so what business does anyone have preaching anything else? Let us no more be distracted by the idols of dogma. Of course, the past is the past; we cannot change it. But the past and present eventually become the future. So let's bury our shameful histories, forgive each other and our own selves, and start from scratch in living the Word.

When the Gospel of John starts, *"In the beginning was the Word, and the Word was with God and the Word was God . . ."* the Word was not the canonized book that you're, I hope, by now, holding in your hand. It is not the Bible that is inerrant and infallible; it is *God* who is inerrant and infallible. The Bible is the miracle that has resulted from the words of the "Ancient of Days," God's word to the world through ages of time that we can only read about because we don't know what exactly happened. We weren't there, and no one today can claim to have been. I don't care how many visions and revelations someone claims to have had. Unlike Joseph Smith claimed, and as Mormons believe, God has never been silent before and since His mortal walk on earth:

> Heaven and earth may pass away, but my words shall
> not pass away.
> Luke 21:33

Like I said before about miracles, past or present, their purpose is clear: *to help us believe.* So the Bible—yes, written by errant and fallible human beings—is about an inerrant, infallible God, the Word made flesh. The Bible is a miracle book containing things that matter to us as human beings, and is the only witness we have or need of Jesus Christ. But the book itself should never be worshipped or revered as anything more, or it is idol worship.

Let me apologize if what I've said has offended you. It has taken a great amount of courage to even suggest some of the things I have. But as Jesus was an unorthodox Jew who literally died so His word could enter your hearts, I pray that my life as a former Mormon turned unorthodox Christian may help you consider simplifying your spiritual lives, clean your spiritual houses, and truly find rest unto your souls.

> With men this is impossible; but with
> God all things are possible.

We are promised that by *human* effort, this is impossible. Read any history book and it would appear this point has been made quite evident. But with God in the common grounds equation, all things are possible. In fact, it's change-the-world possible! So again, I ask that we skip the impossible—obviously been there, done that—and go for the *possible* this time. Now. Today! Let's go for God this time, letting Christ alone into our cleaned out souls as if we are doing it for the very first time—with fresh, new, loving, compassionate hearts, new eyes, open minds, ready and eager with the faith of a child. Let your ears hear, your heart be filled with love, compassion and forgiveness, setting aside any and all preconceived notions, ideas, and beliefs. For the first time, let us listen with new ears to God's answer in Jesus Christ. Because, for the entire world—even the vast majority of those claiming to be Christians—this may very well be the first time.

Unorthodox Christianity: Love God, Love Your Neighbor, Love Your Enemies

And one of the scribes came, and having heard them reasoning together,
and perceiving that he had answered them well, asked him, Which is the first commandment of all?
And Jesus answered him, The first of all the commandments is, Hear, O Israel; The Lord our God is one Lord:
And thou shalt love the Lord thy God with all they heart, and with all thy soul, and with all thy mind, and with all thy strength:
this is the first commandment.
And the second is like, namely this: Thou shalt love thy neighbour as thyself.
There is none other commandment greater than these.
And the scribe said unto him, Well, Master, thou hast said the truth:
for there is one God; and there is none other but He:
And to love him with all the heart, and with all the

understanding, and with all the soul, and with all the
strength, and to love his neighbor as himself,
is more than all whole burnt offerings and sacrifices.
And when Jesus saw that he answered discreetly, he said
unto him, Thou art not far from the kingdom of God.
Mark 12: 28–34

Jesus made it so easy for us to live a life of love and peace, even set the stage by His own ultimate example of God's infinite love for us. The problem has been that no one has wanted to choose love as a solution to conflict—even those professing to be Christians! Our embarrassing history has only shown a path of unsuccessful solutions of war and retaliation. We act offensively and maliciously, reacting in the same manner or worse. The aphorism "love is all you need" is more cliché than a key to peace. But Jesus exhorts love as a commandment that surpasses all commandments:

A new commandment I give unto you,
That ye love one another; as I have loved you,
that ye also love one another.
By this all men know that ye are my disciples,
if ye have love one to another.
John 13:34

It is by *love* that true followers of Christ will be known. So if you claim to be a Christian, show it. Not because you say so. Not by advertising bumper stickers or little fish icons on the back of your vehicle. Not by how many scriptures are memorized, prepped and ready on your tongue, how many Bible studies you've done, nor how long your prayers are. Not by your religious apparel, nor how you dress for church on Sunday. Not by one single tithed dollar, or an accounting thereof. Not by what you eat or don't eat. Not by a degree in theology or religious studies, nor being a card-carrying member of a religion you've kept "from your youth up," like the rich young man who petitioned Jesus.

How shall the world know? By *love*. That's it. Is it really that simple? Yes. So simple it's been so difficult for us to figure out after all this time? Unfortunately, yes. There are so many who claim to be God-fearing Christians who live and act in bigotry, hate and intolerance, completely contrary to what Christ taught. Recognize those kinds of people and, as Jesus said, do not follow after them.

> Take heed that ye do not your alms before men, to be seen of them:
> otherwise ye have no reward of your Father which is in heaven.
> Therefore when thou doest thine alms, do not sound a trumpet before thee, as the hypocrites do in the synagogues and in the streets, that they may have glory of men.
> Verily I say unto you, They have their reward.
> But when thou doest alms, let not thy left hand know what thy right hand doeth.
> That thine alms may be in secret:
> and thy Father which seeth in secret himself shall reward thee openly.
> And when thou prayest, thou shalt not be as the hypocrites are:
> for they love to pray standing in the synagogues and in the corners of the streets, that they may be seen of men.
> Verily I say until you, They have their reward.
> But thou, when thou prayest, enter into thy closet,
> and when thou hast shut thy door, pray to thy Father which is in secret;

and thy Father which seeth in secret shall reward thee openly.

But when ye pray, use not vain repetitions, as the heathen do:

for they think that they shall be heard for their much speaking.

Be not ye therefore like unto them:

for your Father knoweth what things ye have need of, before ye ask Him.

Matthew 6: 1–8

The first and second chapters of this book were entitled "What Shall I Do?" This chapter will begin to answer that question, as Jesus Christ now gives us our first directions on living a life unorthodox:

Love God

Which is the first commandment of all?

And Jesus answered him, The first of all the commandments is,

Hear, O Israel; The Lord our God is one Lord:

And thou shalt **love the Lord thy God** with all they heart,

and with all thy soul, and with all thy mind, and with all thy strength:

this is the first commandment.

Mark 12: 28–34 (bold added)

From the moment we are born as infants into this existence and dimension of time, our innocent reliance on elements greater than ourselves generates more than enough evidence of life purpose. We are not born atheists. In fact, we are not born as anything but human—and our childlike faith could sustain us, if left pure and untainted. Unfortunately, the world is not that kind. Trust can and is often broken by abuse and neglect. Bitterness and loneliness can end up replacing our youthful joys and happiness. And a system of beliefs can overcome the personal, simple faith relationship between the created and Creator.

It is written in the Gospels that Jesus' glorious birth was an immaculate one. I don't know Jesus' mother, Mary. I wasn't there, I never saw her with my own eyes. Neither have you. But after reading and studying the varying positions on the subject of immaculate conception, I know very well that there are some things that are just beyond comprehension. Then again, God has created an infinite amount of things that are beyond comprehension! So based upon my extremely limited comprehension and understanding, I believe that the creation of God in the flesh must have been an incredible, inconceivable miracle before Jesus even took His first human breath. It is recorded that Mary knew this too—knew her purpose. Imagine the parental responsibility! Even though raised in Judaism, Jesus must have been the first and only human being nurtured with a pure, unadulterated faith until the realization of exactly who He was and His life purpose was set before Him. As both mortal and immortal, He truly knew His Father. So good job, Mary and Joseph; you knew and believed in who you were dealing with, enough to humbly raise the very Son of God accordingly!

I don't know if Jesus Christ rose again on the third day. I wasn't there. I didn't see it with my own eyes. Neither have you. However, if common sense were indeed to dictate that an infinite God would prove to the world that He had all control over the elements of time, including *death*, one ultimate sacrifice and one resurrection does it for me. One is a good number. One suits me.

Bottom line, I believe in Jesus Christ, and I'm *done!*

Some may argue that I'm just being reprogrammed by the Bible and fooled by Christian tenets that have been developed over time, that I'm just using the Gospels to support my own way of thinking. You know, I may tend to agree with you—if there hadn't already been two thousand years of the same debates rehashed. Are we not tired of the same points of controversy and doctrines being squabbled over? This is not difficult. Either we believe Jesus Christ is who He said He is, or we do not—it really *is* that plain and simple. His very existence was and is the message appealing to humanity's simple belief and child-like faith:

> " . . . that whosoever believeth in Him should not perish, but have everlasting life."
> John 3:16

I don't know about you, but there came a point when I was *so* ready for some answers from God, whomever or whatever He was. It wasn't until I professed that I truly believed in my Creator enough to inquire about who He was, that Jesus Christ finally revealed Himself to me. My only regret was it took over thirty years, but the regret has since been replaced with purpose and understanding. There was a reason it took that long for me to be born again—at any other time I may not have been ready to take such a life changing step. Only He who has control of all time knew when it was right—and as usual, His timing is impeccable, whether it takes thirty years or two thousand years to get it.

If one does *not* believe in a Creator, both love and purpose have a very difficult time taking root in a soul because belief is the anchor. This is why it's so important to hold fast to that childlike faith and never compromise it to synthetic beliefs. The purpose of all creations, including your own existence, needs to be realized and respected. And the act of loving God can only be accomplished if you first *believe* in Him. Not like perpetuated fantastical icons like Santa Claus, the Easter Bunny, the Tooth Fairy, or Superman—but a true, bona fide belief that you hold on to, like that one precious pearl.

And how could you love God if you deny or refuse to believe His awesome and wondrous existence revealed every second of every day? Amazingly, God made it even easier for the unbeliever. He came in the flesh so you could believe, once and for all, that He is who He said He was:

> "Before Abraham was, I am."
> John 8:58

A personal relationship with God, connected through prayer, knowing that He understands the human condition because He went through it Himself, is the greatest gift of love given to the world. And now it's time to pass it on . . .

Love Your Neighbor

> And the second is like unto it:
> Thou shalt **love thy neighbor** as thyself.
> On these two commandments hang all the law and the prophets.
> Matthew 22: 37–40 (bold added)

Okay, number one: Love God. Number two: Love your neighbor. Everything hangs on these two commandments. Have the societies of the world learned these yet? Actually, I think quite a few of us may still be hung up on commandment number one, loving a God unseen. But the next real hang-up will be the concept of loving our neighbors—people we see every day.

> And who is my neighbor?
> Luke 10:29

The best illustration that can ever be given about loving our neighbors is found in Jesus' parable of the Good Samaritan in Luke 10. Look it up and read it. This is your example of how to treat everyone. I'll comment on this parable later in this chapter.

How do we love? For someone who may be a bit rusty on the concept, it may be somewhat of a challenge. But Christ said, "Love thy neighbor as thyself." How much do you love yourself? If you haven't gotten as far as loving yourself as a creation of God's own hands, then back up a little and master that—learn how to love your Creator, then learn how to love yourself, then apply that same kind of love to others. And if you think that's a challenge, read on . . .

Love Your Enemies

> Ye have heard that it hath been said, Thou shalt love thy neighbour, and hate thine enemy.
>
> But I say unto you, **Love** your enemies, **bless** them that curse you, **do good** to them that hate you, and **pray** for them which despitefully use you, and persecute you;

That he may be the children of your Father which is in heaven: for he maketh his sun to rise on the evil and on the good, and sendeth rain on the just and on the unjust.

For if ye love them which love you, what reward have ye?

Do not even the publicans the same?
And if ye salute your brethren only, what do you more [than others]?

Do not even the publicans so?
Matthew 5: 43–47 (bold added)

Love your enemies. Hmmm. Impossible? With humans at the helm, yes. But with God in the equation, no. I find it interesting that Jesus doesn't just say, "love everyone." He actually recognizes that enemies exist and spells out exactly how we are to treat them: with *love*.

Could you imagine how time would have stood still if America had reacted to the tragedy of 9/11 with forgiveness and love towards Osama bin Laden, the clear enemy? What if the U.S. had asked bin Laden for forgiveness of whatever it was that triggered such deepened hate and despise within him and his followers for believing that they must declare jihad upon us and hurt innocent people in such a horrible way? For us to apologize to bin Laden for any hurt we had caused him, in the ashes of our own tragedy and loss, would have been one of those change the world reactive moments we did not take advantage of. We blew it. We chose to continue war, hate, vengeance, greed and retribution. These don't change a thing. But love, peace and forgiveness could change the world.

Are we getting this yet?

One of the world's great icons of hope in our generation, Mother Teresa, said: "If we really want to love, we must first learn how to forgive." How America's court system would collapse if such a concept as forgiveness were introduced! Would any penalty or sentence be rendered effective? Victims forgiving the perpetrators for the offenses, and perpetrators convicted by their own hearts rather than by a legalistic system, spurring remorse for their deeds. Would forgiveness change the life of either the perpetrator or the victim, or both? Just how successful would forgiveness be in a world like ours? Would the purposes of terrible acts be realized—bad things happening to good people, and vice versa? Maybe, maybe not. I'll tell you right now, the press would be all over something on the magnitude of global forgiveness and love. If we, as true disciples of Christ, could forgive Osama bin Laden for 9/11, instead of falling back on the primitive reactions of war and revenge as our pitiful history has consistently dictated, what would happen? If the American Indians could lay to rest the hurt derived from the genocide of its peoples, Israel and Palestine come together under a truce of peace, the abused forgive their abusers, the divided no longer divided, the hurt no longer hurt, the unloved finally loved—what a global event it would be!

Now, here may be a very difficult concept to grasp. Satan is often referred to as the enemy. If Jesus commands us to love our enemies, and Satan is the biggest of them all, then how are we supposed to treat such an enemy, according to His word? It boggles the mind to think we could react to such an icon of evil with love, but think about it—love is the perfect response! I can't rightly define it as a weapon for combat, but used again and again, love can be a powerful, overwhelming *response* to evil. This is why I believe Jesus said to turn the other cheek and why He did not speak a word in His own defense before being crucified. Don't embrace evil, do not fight evil with evil, don't harbor a heart of stone, stubbornness or revenge—this is what has been happening in the world since the beginning of time, and look where it's gotten us. Instead, react and respond to the inflictions of evil with the *greater power of love*, because that is what will change the world. We already know what the power of hate and division does. Isn't it time to see what the power of love can do?

Love is God's solution to achieving peace. Can we not at least try it out, one last time, before our beautiful world is damaged beyond repair? Just how hard would it be for us to love, bless, do good to and pray for our enemies? The world really wouldn't know because it hasn't been tried. These just aren't things we tend to do in response to those who trespass against us. In fact, they may sound more like impossible challenges than solutions in dealing with people who wish us ill. But with God, it *is* a solution! However, we have to actually try doing it. So from now on let's at least try testing out the possibility of loving our enemies and just see what happens!

Jesus Christ: Miracles and Events

As mentioned in the previous chapter, the events surrounding Christ's birth and death give meaning to many holidays. Belief in these events may or may not be significant to you. Many a well-written novel or story could almost convince belief in pure fantasy. J.R.R. Tolkien's *Lord of the Rings* delves you into the realm of Middle Earth, nearly convincing one that such a world existed—maps are even provided. Homer's *Iliad* and *Odyssey*, both written before Christ was born, are chock full of myth and legend, yet are regarded as works that can tell us a little something about Ancient Greece. The Book of Mormon is a fictional history of the Ancient Americas, and still the LDS church endorses and perpetuates its contents as truth. The Bible is often read out of context and way too literally; this can be dangerous, as scripture can and is often used to excuse some awful atrocities. Excuses that fly right in the face of and contradict Jesus' message of love and peace. What can be drawn out of any book can influence belief and can either edify and enlighten us, or taint or deprive us of that pure, childlike faith that we so desperately need to find inside of ourselves again.

Believe in Me

> Believe me that I am in the Father, and the Father in me:
> Or else believe me for the very works' sake . . .
> John 14:11

Do we believe that Jesus healed the sick, caused the blind to see, the lame to walk, the dead to come alive, fed five thousand, walked on water, and calmed a stormy sea? Do we believe that He was indeed the Messiah, the prophesied God in the flesh who came to connect with humanity for a brief moment in time?

What Christ is saying in the above passage is, if we don't believe Him for who He claims to be, *at least* believe the miracles and at least believe for the sake of what He has shown the world. Even if you haven't believed in anything or anybody for quite some time, or have trust issues, why not take the chance now? For an unbeliever, miracles may not do anything for them one way or another. But the fact is, miracles happen every day—whether you believe in them or not. Miracles surround us, whether we know it or not, whether we can see them or not. So in all actuality, unbelievers have nothing to lose in at least trying to understand their purpose.

But say you do believe that Jesus did these things, and that His miracles and extraordinary events actually do something for you. How much better off would you be had you *not* believed? One can only determine that for one's self, but at *least* take the chance! Take the journey, take the risk. Believe me, you have nothing to lose. It is neither logic nor reason that is lacking in the world today. Both are plentiful in the world today, and neither can nor should be ignored. No, it is our innate faith that is in severe deficit these days—something that logic and reason cannot satisfy in the makeup of the human heart, mind and soul.

It is my hope that one could connect with the miracles and teachings of Jesus Christ, as I had connected with the miracle of the blind man in John 9. Test His teachings personally and privately, with no outside competition for your faith—your one precious pearl.

Jesus Christ: Parables and Teachings

> And the disciples came and said unto him,
> Why speakest thou unto them in parables?
> He answered and said unto them,
> Because it is given unto you to know the mysteries of the kingdom of heaven,
> But to them it is not given . . .
> Therefore speak I to them in parables: because they seeing see not;
> and hearing they hear not, neither do they understand . . .
> For this people's heart is waxed gross, and their ears are dull of hearing,

and their eyes they have closed; lest at any time they should see with their eyes
and hear with their ears, and should understand with their heart,
and should be converted, and I should heal them.
Matthew 13: 10–15

Love God. Love your neighbor. Love your enemies. Three admonitions of love that are the crux of living as an unorthodox Christian in a world of mass confusion. Along with these instructions of love, miraculous events and miracles were performed by Christ to bring about belief among generations of unbelievers.

The parables and teachings of Christ can and most certainly will satisfy your longing for peace and secure that one belief in Him. Simple stories that are timeless, not filled with a lot of lip service and hypocrisy, but actually tell us what we can do to live a life unorthodox to the mainstreams of religion. Knowing that an almighty God came down to teach us in simple parables, in a manner in which the entire world could understand, just shows that He loves us that much more. Here are just a few key ones to get you started:

The Good Samaritan

As mentioned before, one of my favorite parables of Jesus Christ is that of the Good Samaritan (Luke 10: 25–37). This awesome parable has become the representation of how a Christ-like life should be led. This is also our handbook parable as to how to love our neighbors. Our approach towards others should be of unconditional love, our motives being simply to lend a hand to help others who are in trouble. I do understand that, in a world full of treachery, deception and malice, the moral of this parable may, unfortunately, be a little more difficult for us to implement today. We sometimes fear for our own safety in certain situations where we desire to render our assistance. Jesus has also asked us to be as "harmless as doves and as wise as serpents" (Matthew 10:16). We have been created with some important, major organs: the brain and the heart. Use *both*, especially when approaching those in need. But don't just do nothing—do whatever you can. Remember, your actions of love may be the key element that brings purpose to another human being's life, thereby changing the world—one good deed at a time!

The Sower

Versions of this parable can be found in Matthew 13 and Mark 4. I include this timeless parable mainly to gauge now as then how Jesus' words are received. You will see there are many elements that afflict the seed that is sown: some seed becomes bird food, some fall on rocks where they could not take root, some have shallow roots, some are scorched by the sun, or choked by thorns. All of these are ways that pure, innocent faith can be tainted. But some seed falls on good soil, so remember: belief can be solidly anchored. It all depends on what that belief is anchored *to*.

The Prodigal Son

I don't know about you and your religious history but when I left Mormonism, I had some major abandonment issues. How could the "God" and false Christ I had believed in Mormonism for thirty years just no longer exist? Leave me without *anyone*, not even a friend to trust? Why was I raised all those years believing what I did? What was the purpose of *that*? I felt like a fool. Why would God let this kind of pain happen to me? Why should I trust or believe anyone or anything ever again?

It is completely comprehensible that one could turn away from every single belief known to heaven and earth. I didn't trust anyone or anything after I left Mormonism. I couldn't even trust my own family and friends. I thought if Mormonism wasn't true, then nothing was—yet I still yearned for some credibility somewhere, from someone; a little proof that I wasn't alone in a world reeking with hypocrisy and judgment.

Fortunately, God knew this and answered that dare with that powerful solution of unconditional love: No matter what you did, no matter kind of person you've become, no matter what you've been through, *I love you.* You're worth saving. So come on home and let's have a party. Let's celebrate your return to Me. Unconditional love—now, *that's* something worth celebrating!

Wheat and Tares

This is one of a few pivotal parables differentiating belief and unbelief. Check it out in Matthew 13. Whether you are a believer or unbeliever *is* the question here. Let's think about this for a moment: For as much as atheists or anti-Christ religions argue and defend their unbelief, what's the point? In turn, for as much as Jesus-believing Christians such as me attempting to argue and convince others about my belief in Christ, what's the point? No one is going to convince anyone of who's wrong or who's right. It is the people caught in the middle of this battle who I wish to address, because when it comes right down to it, the choice always comes up with the question: *Do you believe?* If you don't, then you don't. If you do, then you do. And this is where we accept this in each other, and grow together until the promised harvest.

I had once considered an atheistic approach to living, realizing that I would have lived in denial more than I ever did in Mormonism. All questions and debates dead ended in the concept of one thing I knew I'd never have, whether an atheist or not: *control.* No one has control of their lives, of time, of the elements. Hurricane Katrina wasn't selective in her destructive path. Earthquakes and tornadoes are random. Death comes to us all. As I said before, we are not born atheists. But just because atheists lack belief doesn't mean they are devoid of faith. Unbelievers in God are subjected to the same elements in the world as believers.

> That ye may be children of your Father which is in heaven
> for he maketh his sun to rise on the evil and on the good,
> and sendeth rain on the just and on the unjust.
> Matthew 5:45

There is an inexplicable, infinite God who is ever mindful of those who do possess that *one* simple belief that shows our love for Him. Can it be afforded? Hopefully, your answer is yes. If not, amazingly—*God understands*. We've all been there at some point in our lives, and with Jesus Christ, we have God's undying patience and unconditional love—an amazing gift called grace. God wants you to choose Him, so what do you have to lose by at least putting Jesus Christ in the running? Your riches? Your life? Your family and friends? Your home? I've been through the needle's eye, and I'm willing to bet that I'm not the only one. Take your time, but please make sure you're not wasting it on dogmatic drivel, pointless arguments or circular logic.

> But many that are first shall be last;
> and the last shall be first.

My next book, *Unorthodox Christianity*, will expound more upon the elements of these last two chapters. Like many things that have become obsolete, the age of religion needs to come to a close because religion hasn't filled the needs of the human spirit. Yes, we've tried. No, it hasn't worked. So it is my hope that both this book and its sequel will help not just Mormons and Christians, but *anyone* who is either stuck or consumed by the confines of their current beliefs have the courage to step over the boundaries and comfort zones with the faith of a child and see the world again with new eyes.

Jesus Christ calls to us as He did two thousand years ago when both Jewish and Roman governments and religions consumed the lives of people He spoke to. He simply asks, now as then, for us to believe in Him. He is the only one who can truly fill the needs of the human spirit, but most of all, give the world what is truly needed—love, peace and rest.

> Peace I leave with you,
> My peace I give unto you:
> Not as the world giveth, give I unto you.
> Let not your heart be troubled,
> Neither let it be afraid.
> John 14: 27

Epilogue

> Behold, we have forsaken all, and followed thee;
> what shall we have therefore?

The age of religion may not yet be over in the rest of the world, but it can be for you. It may be a long haul before the entire world can give up the chains that bind it, but you yourself can quietly usher in for yourself an age of faith. For there is something we all have that is both precious and fleeting—time.

It is worth spending the time for created to meet Creator. There is no better relationship than one that connects with an infinite God who has connected with humanity by experiencing the human condition—living a human life, enjoying human company, working with human hands, seeing through human eyes, shedding human tears, suffering human pain, and ultimately dying a human death. My one belief is that Jesus Christ did all of these things—for me, for you, for the world. The miracle of the created being able to enjoy an infinite God's eternal presence, seeing through healed eyes and living past the portals of death makes Jesus' invitation to be born again surely an offer not to sorrowfully walk away from, as the rich young man did.

If you believe, then you are not far from the kingdom of God, for the treasure that you will inherit is eternal life—which, is it not, *time*? Keep all aspects of your life simple, including your spiritual one.

For what more do you need than what Jesus already offers you in His grace? If your life has gotten out of control, there's absolutely nothing stopping you from starting over. There are far enough complexities and hypocrisies in this world, so much that it has been difficult to just engage in the simple, good precepts of Christ. Why? There is so much religious clutter we don't know where to begin, so make Jesus' simple teachings as complex as you get. By doing so, you'll be ahead of the majority that follows the broad, wide paths of organized religion.

> No man can serve two masters.
> For either he will hate the one and love the other,
> or hold on to the one, and despise the other.
> Ye cannot serve God and mammon.
> Matthew 6:24

I made choices that resulted in saying goodbye to both Mormonism and mainstream Christianity. An exchange of an old life for a new, a bubble burst by a needle that eventually swung wide the doors of truth. They were not easy choices, but they were the right ones for me. Former masters that ruled over thirty years of my life no longer had a grip upon me. The Master of truth had set me free.

Has it been a difficult journey? At times, yes. I can't say that thirty years were wasted, but I do regret wasting time not learning the lessons I should have. I believe one of the greatest gifts given to humankind is the freedom of choice. The true freedom to search for purpose in life, in death and beyond what we claim we see is what true free agency is. That freedom led me to new life. All I had to do was ask, and the journey began. All I had to do was seek, and the path unfolded. All I had to do was knock, and the doors of purpose swung wide open to reveal a life ahead of me—a life filled with a much needed peace and rest.

> Ask and ye shall receive,
> Seek and ye shall find.
> Knock, and it shall be opened unto you.
> Matthew 7:7

Look back at your own life and learn from your past. You have purpose; your past can help you to see the new paths and choices ahead of you, to see the only one who can save you, like that rich young man who approached the Good Master. Most of all, look forward to the new paths ahead of you as time, destiny and purpose lay before you—no matter where you are, no matter what kind of life you've lived before, no matter what the world thinks of you. Once through the needle's eye, don't be wasting time going back through it! Always remember what you've learned:

> And ye now therefore have sorrow:
> But I will see you again, and your heart shall rejoice,
> And your joy no man taketh from you.
>
> And in that day ye shall ask me nothing.
> Verily verily, I say unto you,
> Whatsoever ye shall ask the Father in my name, he will give you.
>
> Hitherto have ye asked nothing in my name:
> Ask, and ye shall receive, that your joy may be full.
> John 16: 22–24

Reach up, grab His hand—and this time, *don't let go*.

Glossary of LDS Terminology

13 Articles of Faith

The thirteen basic statements of LDS belief, similar in purpose to the Nicene Creed, but instead based upon Mormon doctrine.

Apostate

One who both leaves the church and turns their back on the religion.

Baptism

There are three types of baptisms in the Mormon church: covenant baptisms, convert baptisms and baptisms for the dead. Covenant baptisms happen when a child reaches the age of eight years old, known as the age of accountability. Convert baptisms result from those who wish to convert to Mormonism. Baptisms for the dead are proxy baptisms conducted only in the temple.

Book of Mormon

A book counted among the LDS scriptures, purportedly translated by Joseph Smith from gold plates. The book claims to be a history of Israelites who migrated to the Americas, therefore claiming to reveal the derivation of American Indian tribes. The book also claims that Jesus Christ appeared in the Americas after his ascension. Hence, the LDS church calls the book Another Testament of Jesus Christ. The book is considered true by Mormons, and is the crux of their religion. See LDS *Quad*.

Brigham Young
Second president/prophet of the Mormon church, after Joseph Smith.

Brigham Young University
An LDS university located in Provo, Utah. There are also BYU Hawaii and BYU Idaho, formerly Ricks College in Rexburg.

Calling
A job or position in the church. An LDS member cannot choose their callings. Only the bishop, stake president or higher priesthood authority can call a member to a job or position in the church.

Doctrine and Covenants
A book mainly containing the revelations of Joseph Smith. It is considered scripture and a part of the LDS Quad. See LDS *Quad*.

The *Ensign*
One of the main monthly LDS magazine publications.

Eternal progression/perfection
The life and path of an active LDS member, as delineated by the doctrines and ordinances of the Mormon religion. The purpose and goal is for Mormons to become gods of their own worlds. Lorenzo Snow, fifth LDS prophet, coined the following aphorism: "As man is, God once was—as God is, man may become."

Fast and Testimony meeting
Held the first Sunday of the month. LDS members fast for two meals. The entire service is dedicated to members bearing their testimonies to the rest of the congregation. See *Testimony*.

Fireside
Another LDS meeting that generally focuses on one topic. Smaller firesides, like youth firesides, can be held in members' homes. Ward, stake or larger firesides are usually held in the ward buildings or stake centers.

First Presidency
The president/prophet of the church and his two counselors—the highest priesthood position in the LDS church.

General Authorities
LDS church leaders under the First Presidency in the priesthood hierarchy. These include the apostles, the seventies, presiding bishopric, etc.

Home Teachers
Priesthood holders (men) who are assigned to visit members' homes once per month for the purpose of checking up on the needs of the family and to give a short message/lesson. See *Visiting Teachers*.

Improvement Era:
An early LDS publication, no longer exists.

Inactive
The status of a member of the church who doesn't go to church regularly.

Homemaking meeting
One night a month where members of the Relief Society get together to learn various homemaking skills.

Jesus Christ (of Mormonism)
The Jesus Christ of Mormonism is not God in the flesh. God the Father and Jesus are two separate beings. Joseph Smith claimed to have seen two separate beings in his vision. The Jesus Christ of Mormonism is the Jesus of the Book of Mormon, not of the Bible.

Joseph Smith
First president/prophet and founder of Mormonism.

LDS
Acronym for Latter-day Saint (Mormon).

LDS Quad/Scriptures
Canon of LDS scripture comprised of: The KJV Bible with Joseph Smith Translation footnotes, Book of Mormon, Doctrine and Covenants, and Pearl of Great Price.

Member
A member of the LDS church. There are varying statuses of membership including: inactive and non-member; part member, as well as New Order Mormons, Jack Mormons, etc.

Mormon, Mormonism
A character in the Book of Mormon, from which the term Mormonism was derived.

Missionaries
LDS men, who turn nineteen years old, go into what is called the mission field for two years for the sole purpose of converting people to Mormonism. They are heavily programmed on a campus in Provo,

Utah, called the Missionary Training Center, or MTC. The First Presidency "calls" each young man to their mission. See *Callings*.

Mutual
A name for the LDS youth program. See *Young Women/Young Men*.

Non-Member
A term used by Mormons in reference to those who are not a member of the LDS church.

Pearl of Great Price
Another book of scripture containing the translations of Joseph Smith, purportedly derived from Egyptian papyri. It also contains a self-authored history of Joseph Smith. See LDS *Quad*.

President/Prophet
The head of the LDS church, the "mouthpiece of God" (much like Catholicism's Pope).

Priesthood
According to Mormon doctrine, the "power of God on earth." Only men can hold the priesthood, which is divided into two categories: the Aaronic priesthood, known as the lesser priesthood, is bestowed upon teenage boys once they turn twelve years old. This priesthood is divided into quorums of deacons, teachers and priests. The higher priesthood, called the "Melchizedek" priesthood, is bestowed upon young men usually before they go on their missions. This priesthood is divided into quorums consisting of elders, high priests, seventies, patriarchs and apostles.

Primary
Children's organization, for ages 3 to 11.

Relief Society
Women's organization.

Reorganized Church of Jesus Christ of Latter-day Saints (RLDS)
A denominational splinter of Mormonism founded by Joseph Smith III, son of Joseph Smith. The RLDS, now known as the "Community of Christ" still consider the Book of Mormon and Doctrine and Covenants as scripture. They have their own prophet and organized leadership.

Returned Missionary
A young man who has come home or "returned" after honorably serving an LDS mission.

Sacrament Meeting
LDS Sunday services held in the wards.

Sealed
A temple ritual during which family members are "sealed" together for eternity. If a couple is married in the temple, they have formed the covenant for their family, which means their children will be "born under the covenant." If a family converts to Mormonism, they can eventually be sealed in the temple; I believe that they must be active members for at least a year. An adopted child can be sealed in the temple to a Mormon family. There are also sealings for the dead by proxy.

Seminary
A study program for LDS youth focusing upon LDS scriptures.

Stake
A church organizational unit comprised of a dozen or so wards (see "Wards") headed by a Stake Presidency. Several Stakes comprise an Area. An Area is headed by an Area Presidency. There are a few dozen Areas in the entire world; when I was a Mormon, there were no areas, only Regions headed by regional representatives.

Temple, Temple Covenants
Edifice where only those Mormons found worthy and given a recommend by their bishop can attend. Rituals and covenantal ordinances are performed there for both the living and the dead by proxy.

Testimony
A statement made by Mormons that portrays their individual beliefs in the LDS church. Testimonies are programmed into children from a very early age—this is the main reason why their testimonies sound pretty much the same (i.e. "I want to bear my testimony that I know this church is true, the Book of Mormon is true, Joseph Smith was a prophet, I love my family . . ."). LDS missionaries also use their testimonies in conversion efforts, especially to direct the discussions. Many Mormons are taught that they should strengthen and bear their testimonies for times when they don't quite know what to say, if their faith is shaken, or if they are feeling persecuted.

Tithing/Tithing Settlement
Tithing is a required donation of ten percent of members' incomes, as one cannot go to the temple if they don't pay their tithing. Tith-

ing settlement occurs at the end of the year, in December, when members are held accountable for their tithed.

Visiting Teachers
Members of the Relief Society (women) who are assigned to visit the homes of women in the church once per month for the purpose of checking up on the woman's needs and to give a short message or lesson. See *Home Teachers*.

Ward
A church organizational unit comprised of a local congregation of LDS members. A ward is headed by a ward bishopric. Several wards comprise a Stake. See *Stake*.

Willie and Martin Handcart Companies: The "Second Rescue"
In 1856 the Willie and Martin Handcart Companies were stranded near the Continental Divide in a bitter Wyoming winter. The Riverton Wyoming stake, in my home town, were the ones which did the Mormon "temple work" for the dead that were a part of those handcart companies, which is known as the Second Rescue.

Word of Wisdom
Mormonism's code of health, which excludes alcohol, illegal drugs, tobacco usage and caffeine (coffee, black tea, power drinks, etc. *Note: Since I haven't been a Mormon since the whole string of energy/power drinks have come out, I'm also assuming this also includes them, but I'm not sure what has been said in the LDS circuits)*. You cannot go to the temple if you do not obey the Word of Wisdom.

Young Women/Young Men
LDS teenage youth organization.